As We Say In Our House

As We Say In Our House

– A Book of Family Sayings –

NIGEL REES

 Robson Books

Special edition for PAST TIMES

As We Say In Our House
text © Nigel Rees

9 8 7 6 5 4 3 2 1

PAST TIMES

Contents

Speak, you who are older, for it is fitting that you should, but with accurate knowledge, and do not interrupt the music.

Ecclesiasticus 32:3

Introduction

When I was a little boy, my family went for the summer holiday to a small seaside resort called Llanfairfechan in North Wales. When walking in the hills nearby, I am told that I made a suggestion as to the route we should take. You see, there was this field with a bull in it, and it was my considered opinion that we should go through that field, bull or no bull. 'Why not?' I asked innocently – no doubt aware that not to go through the field with the bull in it would require a substantial detour.

Family history does not record whether my challenging suggestion was, in fact, taken up. What I do know is that the incident is a copper-bottomed example of a family saying in the very act of coinage. From that moment, whenever one member of our family was judged to be rubbing up another the wrong way (me with regard to my elder brother, for example), the expression would be duly trotted out: **'Don't go through a field with a bull in it.'** Since leaving home, I have occasionally been tempted to address these words to anyone I encountered who was tempting providence in some way. But I have refrained, fearing they would not understand what I was talking about and knowing for certain that they would not appreciate the peculiar resonance the saying has for me.

As families go, I do not think that ours had that many special sayings of its own, though I do recall the (possibly unusual) instance of our adopting another family's saying for our own use. As it happens, we heard about this one when we were on a rare summer holiday in *South* Wales – at Penarth, I think. Many such sayings are pretty impenetrable to outsiders but this one appealed to us because of its obvious usefulness. These people that we met explained that if ever anything unaccountable happened in their house – something went missing or went wrong – then, rather than worry too much about the culprit – the explanation invariably advanced was: **'Oh, it's Ivor...'** A very useful person to have about the house, this non-existent Ivor. We took to blaming the same poor, hapless fellow.

The usefulness of these two family expressions should be obvious, but our family also had catchphrases that were just rather silly and served only to revive memories of shared experiences.

And so, what do these examples from my native hearth tell us? If a catchphrase – in the public, often showbusiness, sense – is simply a phrase that has caught on, then a family saying is a phrase or saying that has only caught on within a relatively small circle. A family saying is, if you like, a domestic catchphrase. It may be a form of words that is non-sensical to outsiders. Or it may be a well-known phrase or saying that has a special meaning for members of the family that uses it. Curiously, for words of such apparently limited circulation, family sayings often have their counterparts in other families, even if they are not used in exactly the same way. And people do seem to have a genuine interest in the odd phraseology of households other than their own.

Such, at least, is what I have discovered since I started asking about such matters in the BBC Radio quiz-anthology *Quote... Unquote.* Since introducing the feature in 1989, during the programme's 14th annual series, I have seen it become a firm favourite with listeners. Guest panellists, on the other hand, usually approach the spot with some hesitation, fearing, I suppose, that revealing their own family sayings would be of little interest or benefit to any- body else. But when I ask, 'Was there something that your mother or father *always* used to say?' or 'Is there something you find yourself always saying to your children?', it doesn't usually take long before the reminiscences begin to flow. The panellists are often quite surprised by the reception that their revelations are accorded.

All this prompts listeners to write in with their own contributions. Although many of the sayings are unique to particular families, there is nevertheless a large body of catchphrases common to many families but which is little explored by conventional catchphrase collections. Hence this book. It seeks to celebrate a warm, folksy, homely, nostalgic area of popular speech which, as one correspondent pointed out to me, surely needs to be recorded 'because it is so easily lost or forgotten'. In addition, the book also explores the related fields of 'personal mottoes' – the things you say to yourself to keep your spirits up; 'peculiar proverbs' – especially the near meaningless ones that are sometimes invoked in the home; 'household names' – given to pets and household objects; 'nannyisms' – which have moved into the mainstream; and 'riddles' – especially nonsense ones.

While collecting material for this book, I have been intrigued to find that the phenomenon of family sayings has not been ignored by students of language. Especially is this the case with 'paroemiologists' or people who study proverbs. Many family sayings are proverbs, though just as many are not – in that they do not pretend to embody any general truth. They are merely expressions that have achieved proverbial status within the family.

What a pity it is, incidentally, that the terms 'proverb' and 'proverbial expression' sound so alike but are not really the same sort of thing at all. The proverb has to express a truth. A proverbial saying may be no more than a noise that groups of people have used for some time without any general truth or meaning of wider application being attached to it. Accordingly, in an article entitled 'A Case Study and Analysis of Family Proverb Use' for *Proverbium Yearbook of International Proverb Scholarship* (Volume 8, 1991), Valerie Bornstein distinguished between 'General Proverbs', 'Family Proverbs' and 'Family Sayings'. Here 'Family Proverbs' are proverbs which are similar to 'General Proverbs' but are somehow tied to a family's history. Bornstein defines the somewhat different 'Family Sayings' as being sayings that, unlike proverbs, 'are not used to persuade or give advice or comfort'. She goes on: 'The force or weight these sayings carry is an anecdotal force, known only to members of that family. These sayings may be . . . lost or unexplainable to future members of the family.' Additionally, in 'Family Expressions' in *A Celebration of American Family Folklore* (eds Zeitlin, Kotkin & Baker, 1982), it is suggested that these sayings, 'affirm the ties of shared experience . . . [and] . . . family history.'

Valerie Bornstein gives this example: '[An informant] told me about a little girl that her family knew, who at about five years of age was riding her pony when it suddenly threw her off. Everyone ran to see if she was hurt, but before they arrived she jumped up, grabbed the pony's bridle, said **"All right you son of a bitch, we're gonna try this again"**, and she got back on the pony. This saying has stayed in her family for twenty-five years and has subsequently been used for a multitude of situations that require determination, but only by those family members and friends who were present at the original occasion.'

I am most grateful to all those listeners to BBC Radio *Quote. . . Unquote* and viewers of Channel 4/Yorkshire TV *Countdown* who have offered their family sayings for general scrutiny. Their names are given – together with those of people who have been my guests on the programmes and whose contributions are reproduced here – alongside the particular saying in the text.

In the notes that I have supplied to most of the sayings, I have used the following abbreviations when citing authorities:

Apperson: G L Apperson, *English Proverbs and Proverbial Phrases*, 1929

CODP: *The Concise Oxford Dictionary of Proverbs*, 1982

ODP: *The Oxford Dictionary of Proverbs* (3rd ed), 1970

OED2: *The Oxford English Dictionary* (2nd ed), 1989, (CD-ROM version), 1992

Partridge/*Catch Phrases*:
    Eric Partridge, *A Dictionary of Catch Phrases* (2nd ed, edited by Paul Beale), 1985

Partridge/*Slang*:
    Eric Partridge, *A Dictionary of Slang and Unconventional English* (8th ed, edited by Paul Beale), 1984

I am most grateful to Paul Beale, in particular, for allowing me to quote from material he has acquired since the last two books were published.

My Mother Said I Never Should

It is at our mother's knee, or thereabouts, that we are first introduced to the mysteries of the spoken word. One of the great ironies of life is that those phrases we loathe to hear as youngsters so readily spring from our own lips when, in the fullness of time, we become – in particular – mothers. I am thinking of such wonderful admonitions as, 'It's time you settled down', especially when coupled with ' . . . and found a nice sensible job like your father's.' All mothers of teenage children are likely to say, at some stage, 'You treat this house like a hotel.' I know mine did. The 'things that mother said' are legion, and here they are:

'Heavens, eleven o'clock and not a whore in the house dressed'

When Derrick Carter of Southwold wrote to the radio show to tell us about an unusual saying of *his* mother's, he cannot have foreseen the wave of nostalgia he was precipitating. Whenever her domestic programme was falling behind badly, Mr Carter remembered, his mother would say, regardless of the time: 'Heavens, eleven o'clock and not a whore in the house dressed!' But where had she got this expression from? Mr Carter remarked that both his parents were keen theatregoers in the 1920s and 30s, and he wondered if his mother might have been quoting a line from a play – though whether one can imagine such a sentiment getting past the blue pencil of the Lord Chamberlain's Office in the days of stage censorship is a different matter.

What is interesting about this expression is that, whereas most 'family sayings' are incomprehensible to outsiders, this one was known to many more *Quote...Unquote* listeners. Mona Howard of Hampstead said she believed the full version was, rather: 'Heavens, eleven o'clock and not a whore in the house dressed, not a po emptied, and the streets full of Spanish sailors...' Jo Smithies of Newport, Isle of Wight, recalled the maternal: 'Heavens! four o'clock and not a whore washed and the street full of sailors.' Christopher J Anderson of Cobham came up with *his* mother's subtly different, 'Heavens! Ten o'clock! Not a bed made, not a po emptied, not a whore in the house dressed, and the Spanish soldiers in the courtyard!' Miss M L Fountain of Wembley passed on to us that her brother recalled it, not as a mother's saying, but as something he heard in his days in the Navy, in the form: 'Ten o'clock already – no pos emptied, no beds made and a street full of matelots.'

F H Loxley of Frampton Cotterell, Bristol, dated from 1944 his first hearing of the cry (in the Army): 'Eight o'clock, and not a whore in the house washed and a troopship in the bay.' Vemon Joyner of Maresfield, on the other hand, settled for: 'Eleven o'clock, not a whore washed, not a bed made, and the Japanese fleet in town!'

Turning, as we do, to the works of Eric Partridge, we find that he only once turned his linguistic attention to the comparatively simple phrase 'eleven o'clock and no pos emptied' – though 'no potatoes peeled' and 'no babies scraped' are mentioned as variants. In Paul Beale's revision of Partridge/*Catch Phrases*, there is a 1984 reference to the version used by Terry Wogan on his breakfast radio show (after giving a time-check) – '[It's eight twenty-five]... and

not a child in the house washed.'

The 'whores/pos/sailors' version is possibly a colourful elaboration of this basic expression. But how do so many people know it? Perhaps, after all, one *can* imagine it having escaped the stage censor's blue pencil. One could certainly imagine a pantomime dame attempting something similar. In the 1980s, the comedian Les Dawson in drag is reliably reported to have uttered the 'no pos emptied' line. Rupert Hart-Davis in *The Lyttelton-Hart-Davis Letters* (Vol 3, 1981) writes in a letter dated 9 June 1958: 'In the words of the harassed theatrical landlady, "Half-past four, and not a po emptied".' Whether all or part of the expression is a quotation from a play, or not, one does keep on being drawn back to a possible theatrical origin.

'You should have thought of that before'

Sir Peter Hall, the theatre director, provisionally entitled his memoirs *You Should Have Thought of That Before* – one of the things that his mother always used to say to her only child. 'She was a great one for Suffolk aphorisms,' Hall told the *Observer* (24 May 1992). 'She constantly worried about the risks I took. She thought I was a terrible gambler.' When the autobiography was eventually published (in 1993), it was called *Making an Exhibition of Myself*, based – apparently – on yet another of Hall's mother's admonitions.

'They'd spoil another pair'

'I recall a particular saying of my Mother's which I have never heard voiced by anyone else,' wrote Margaret Baker of Oxley, Wolverhampton. 'If ever she met up with a couple of rather unattractive appearance – ie husband and wife or newly engaged pair – she would invariably say with a resigned air – "Oh, well – they'd spoil another pair".'

Compare the illustrious remark that Samuel Butler made about Thomas and Jane Carlyle (in a letter to Miss E M A Savage, on 21 November 1884): 'It was very good of God to let Carlyle and Mrs Carlyle marry one another and so make only two people miserable instead of four...'

'Ugly enough to eat oats'

'My mother - now gone from us - used to say of startlingly ill-favoured people that they were "ugly enough to eat oats". Very expressive, I think, but I never asked her if this was an original expression' – John Francis, Southampton.

Presumably a variation of 'has a face like a horse'.

'I wouldn't fancy him baked'

On the same theme, W S Hardy of Newton Stewart, Wigtownshire, remembered: 'If my mother saw what appeared to be a mismatched couple together, she would

say, "I don't know what she sees in him – I wouldn't fancy him baked."'

'And a bitch – two afternoons!'

'My mother, born in 1872, once told me that her mother, whenever a family member said something like, "Well, every dog has his day," would mutter this response' – wrote Clare Meadmore of Mount Hawke, Cornwall.

Apperson finds this proverbial addition occurring by 1896 and – earlier, by 1864 – the 'Essex saying', 'Every dog has his day, and a cat has two Sundays.'

'Don't you pour that tea, there will be ginger twins!'

'My mother had some curious but firmly held beliefs. The person who had made the tea, had to pour it. If it was poured by another it would bring ginger twins into the family. The reasoning behind this has baffled me all my life – though mother would hardly have welcomed twins of any colour, having already got a family of ten children' – Emily Howe, Bury St Edmunds, Suffolk.

There are, in fact, several superstitions concerning the pouring out of tea, especially if it involves two people. One is that it is bad luck for two people to pour out of a pot. Another (recounted in the journal *Folklore*, 1940) is this: 'I have often heard...that two women should not catch hold of a teapot at once or one of them will have ginger-headed twins within the year.'

'You'd laugh to see your mother's nose on fire!'

'If I was acting silly, laughing at nothing, this was what my mother would say. I thought this very unfair because I was sure I would not...' – Mrs P Hogan, London N2.

'You're as hopeless as Percy Topliss!'

'If I did anything silly, this is what my mother used to say. Another saying was that someone was, "as daft as a penny watch"' – Kathleen Smith, Keith, Banffshire.

'Have a good cry, get it out of your system'

Lesley Prosser of Builth Wells, Powys, wrote: 'My mother used to say to me, when I was a child, bumped or scraped myself, and wanted to cry, "Be brave, don't cry." So I decided that I would love my little ones better whenever they needed it! And my comfort phrase became, "Have a good cry, get it out of your system." Until one day I was comforting my then 13-year-old daughter after a nasty tumble, with my special phrase, and, between sobs, in puzzled tones, she asked: "*Why* do you *always* say, 'Have a good cry, get it out of your sister...?'"'

'All over the place like a mad woman's under-clothes'

The writer Germaine Greer recalled that, when she was growing up in Australia, her mother's phrase – describing, say, an untidy room – was, 'all over the place like a mad woman's under-clothes'. In consequence, Germaine Greer used *The Mad Woman's Underclothes* as the title of a book of her assorted writings.

Partridge/*Slang* does not find this precise expression but in discussing the phrase 'all over the place like a mad woman's shit' points to the euphemistic variants cited by G A Wilkes in *A Dictionary of Australian Colloquialisms* (1978): '...like a mad woman's knitting...custard...lunch box'. So, Australian it very much seems to be.

When asked what she was cooking for dinner, Mrs Greer would invariably reply: 'Stewed eels and slow poison.'

'A place for everything and everything in its place'

The writer Charles Osborne (who also grew up in Australia) remembered being an untidy child and his mother's nannyish admonition, 'A place for everything and everything in its place' (and quite a well-known saying it is, too – Samuel Smiles quotes it in *Thrift*, 1875).

'Apples don't grow on trees'

'A remark of my mother's which became a family saying: she had bought some particularly delicious apples and my brother and I (children at the time) were eating these at such a rate that she felt obliged to point out, "Apples don't grow on trees, you know!" I should add that my mother was an intelligent and witty woman and knew what she was saying' – Tony Bremner, London N3.

'First up . . . best dressed'

'My mother came from a large family and this was always her saying' – Mrs Smitten, Orpington.

'We shall have to eke it out'

'My mother brought us up – a family of six boys – in the hard times of the 1930s. When the food supply ran low, she would say, "We shall have to eke it out – as the girl did her manners"' – A G Foot, Melton Constable, Norfolk.

'Well, never mind – it won't eat anything'

Margaret Coles of Leeds: 'If ever one of the family received a less than delightful present, or bought something which, when brought home, did not quite match, my mother would say...'

'It will all be the same in a hundred years' time'

Professor Richard L Gregory remembered that this is what his mother would say to him when, as a little boy, he said anything silly. Now, he disapproves of this check on originality.

It is a quite widely known put-down. As 'It will all be one in a hundred/thousand years', it was recorded in various

versions between 1611 and 1839. Bill Wilkes told Paul Beale (1994) that his mother, originally from Norfolk, used the expression 'By that time you'll all be dead and your arse cold' in the same sense.

Compare Samuel Johnson's excellent advice for putting a distressful situation in perspective: 'Consider, Sir, how insignificant this will appear a twelvemonth hence' (Boswell's *Life of Johnson*, for 6 July 1763).

'Wait and See pudding'

Mrs Tickner of West Byfleet, Surrey, was 84 in 1994, and wrote: 'Here are a few my Mum used to say to us children all them years ago. "Mum, what have we for pudding?" – "Wait and See Pudding," said Mum.

'"Mum, these crusts are so hard" – "Harder when there are none, my dear."'

'Accustom the body...'

The writer John Julius Norwich remembered that his mother

(Lady Diana Cooper) could not abide whingeing, whining children and consequently brought him up to be as tough as possible. If a difficulty or unpleasantness of any kind arose, she would advise him to 'accustom the body to...wasps, nettles, bores, or whatever it was'.

John Julius said that his mother would also quote at him a phrase from Hilaire Belloc's poem about 'Lord Hippo'. 'If I was trying to guess something, my mother would say, "Don't guess, Lucy." Apparently, this went back to Mr Baldwin, the Prime Minister, when he was doing *The Times* crossword with his wife, Lucy. He would say it if she was making wild surmises.'

'Oh, she was always like that...'

Liz Smelt of Hurstpierpoint, West Sussex, wrote: 'I only heard this once, but it gives me huge pleasure! After many years in England, my English father died and my Scots Mama returned to Dundee, her original home town, and caught up with lots of wayback friends. On one of these occasions, a friend said something pretty snide, and when I commented later, my Mum said: "Oh, she was always like that – had a boat of her own at the Flood!"'

'In and out – like a dog at a fair'

The mother of Max Stafford-Clark, the theatre director, came from Nottinghamshire and 'kept a very clean house', as he put it. 'We used to have to take our shoes off when we came in the door, if she'd done the cleaning that day. If we'd been in and out of the back door more than twice in a morning, she would say, "Either in or out – you're like a dog at a fair."' Stafford-Clark wondered if this was a local expression. Well, his mother was not alone in using it and, in fact, it is a quotation from R H Barham's poem 'The Jackdaw of Rheims', published with *The Ingoldsby Legends* in 1840. The eponymous bird busies itself on the Cardinal's table:

> In and out
> Through the motley rout,
> That little jackdaw kept hopping about:
> Here and there,
> Like a dog at a fair,
> Over comfits and cates [dainties],
> And dishes and plates...

Barham seems, however, to have been using an already established expression. Apperson finds 'As sprites in the haire, Or dogges in the ffayre' by 1520. In 1893, G L Gower's *Glossary of Surrey Words* had the version: 'They didn't keep nothing reg'lar, it was all over the place like a dog at a fair.'

Compare the expression widely used in similar circumstances – rushing around 'like a fart in a colander'. Partridge/*Catch Phrases* suggests an origin some time in the 1920s. This is also used when describing someone particularly evasive or slippery. Mrs J Harrison of Llanfyllin, Powys, wrote that, as she knew it, the phrase was used to describe someone who was indecisive and the complete version was: 'He's like a fart in a colander – can't make up his mind which hole to come out of!'

'Knobs and chairs and pump-handles'

Mrs Harrison (as above) said that this was her mother's reply to 'our daily demands of "What's for dinner, Mum?" The vision of this has always fascinated me. Mum said her father always used to say it.'

'Up and down like a fiddler's elbow'

Ray Dudley of Walthamstow, London E17: 'Mum, exasperated with her small son (me) who would keep running in and out and chasing up and down stairs – "Stay put, dammit. Up and down like a fiddler's elbow."'

Indeed, 'like a fiddler's elbow' was quite a general expression and had been recorded by 1887. Martin Ward of Diss, Norfolk, commented: 'The richness of this simile is its more metaphorical (and more common) use. I have always heard it used to describe something which is *not* in motion – for instance, the uneven ridge of a house – something which deviates from the horizontal plane.

'Other builders' expressions include: "Hard as a whore's heart" (eg concrete, wood) and, for things which do actually move up and down, "Up and down like a whore's drawers."'

'Caught her foot in the sheet'

The singer and composer Betty Roe told me that her mother when talking of someone who had 'slipped up' (ie become pregnant) would say: 'She must have caught her foot in the sheet.'

'Well, now then, sir, Miss Bankhead'

Carol Williamson of Huntly, Scotland, recalled that her mother (raised on American radio in the 1930s) used to say this regularly. 'Obviously the Miss Bankhead was the original Tallulah but whose catchphrase was it? I think it might have been Meredith Willson who wrote the play *The Music Man.*'

Indeed. Thomas Millstead of Chicago wrote: 'The phrase was used by the composer and orchestra leader Meredith Willson on actress Tallulah Bankhead's radio program *The Big Show* (mid to late 1940s). It was called "big" because it was a one and one-half-hour variety show, very long for radio in those days. Mr Willson (who later wrote the famous Broadway show *The Music Man*) led the orchestra and also had many speaking opportunities. Miss Bankhead, of course, had an exceptionally deep voice. Thus Mr Willson's frequently addressing her as "sir". On *The Big Show*, he also employed a choral group that interacted with him by speaking conversationally instead of singing. He called this act "Meredith Willson and His Talking People".'

'You could guess horse muck twice'

A J Finn of Hedon, Hull: 'One of my late mother's favourite sayings, when asked a question to which she thought the answer was fairly obvious, was, "You could guess 'oss-muck twice, and be right third time!"' I don't know where it came from originally, but it is what she would have described as "a good old Yorkshire expression".'

'Nothing will come of nothing'

The actress Sian Phillips said: 'My mother had a distressing habit of quoting from the more morbid plays of Shakespeare, as in, "What have you got hidden in your satchel?" "Nothing." "Nothing will come of nothing. Speak again."

'And she had a terribly depressing habit of saying, "This too will pass", but I think all mothers say this – I've caught myself saying it to my daughters. But there was another saying I only discovered the source for the other day. It's apparently the last words of Samuel Butler – words uttered on his deathbed. I didn't know this for years. But in moments of tension in the family when things might be going badly wrong, someone would say, "Have you got the cheque-book, Alfred?"'

'Up in Annie's room behind the clock'

My wife recalled her mother using this phrase in the 1950s. Colleen Spittles of Deal, Kent, preferred, 'Up in Annie's room behind the wallpaper' for when 'something had disappeared, who knows where.'

Partridge/*Slang* simply has 'Up in Annie's room' as a services' catchphrase from before the First World War, in reply to a query concerning someone's whereabouts. Partridge/*Catch Phrases* has 'Up in Annie's room behind the clock' as the civilian version of this.

'Like a donkey eats strawberries'

My mother-in-law – or so I am reliably informed by someone better placed to know – used to say this when describing how someone was extremely enthusiastic about something (and not just food). She came from Buckingham-shire and it may be a local expression.

'You can always look down and pick nothing up'

'My mother was very fond of saying this – it usually meant, "Try to better yourself rather than take the easy option"' – R Dixon, Colwich, Staffordshire.

Partridge/*Slang* has this as 'You can always stoop and pick up nothing!' and considers it mostly of Cockney use and a 'remark made by a friend after a "row" or by a parent concerning a child's intended husband (or wife)'.

'It was cheaper than not having it'

The mother of the theatre director Patrick Garland was, he said, a great searcher out of second-hand book bargains. Thus she would often buy books she already had or didn't really want at all. But, as she rationalized it, 'It was cheaper than not having it.'

'That has been clean long enough'

John Craster of Market Lavington, Wiltshire, wrote: 'My mother, Jean Craster, not infrequently said, "Darling, that jumper (or whatever else) has been clean long enough." I find myself saying it to my children and grandchildren.'

'I've got one of the right ones this time'

Sir David Attenborough, the broadcaster, said: 'I had two brothers and we used to have a room in which we sort of, I suppose, used to *carry on*. We used to make a hell of a row, and we used to quarrel and one thing and another, and when it got too bad, my mother used to come in and she used to hit all three of us round the ear, "Clip-clip-clip". And then she used to say, "There you are. I've got one of the right ones this time!"'

'Fetch me something to hit you with'

Fred Ritchie of Pickering, North Yorkshire, wrote: 'When a child was naughty, a friend's mother (a real Yorkshire woman) would say, "Fetch me something to hit you with." I use it myself now, I'm afraid, quite often.'

'I'll just go and empty the ashtrays'

I Moore of Manchester wrote: 'We lived in a terraced house, with no inside toilet or hot water, and when my mother was going to make the beds, she armed herself with a bucket and said, "I'll just go and empty the ashtrays."'

'Always wanted the Big Toy'

Jackie Claridge of Pewsey, Wiltshire, wrote: 'My mother and grandmother always used to say about women who had affairs: "She always wanted the Big Toy...and all the little play things."'

'Ask your father what he's doing, and tell him to stop it'

A frequent injunction, apparently, from the mother of the poet Michael Rosen. She also had a general slogan: 'Don't pick it, wash it.'

'It'll be in the last place you look'

Tony Hawks, the comedian, said: 'I was bombarded with lots of little phrases and sayings when I was little, and none of them seemed to make any sense at all. If my mother said, "Tony, go and tidy your room" and I said "I can't. I've got to go and play football", she'd say, "I'll go and play football you, if you're not careful." I just got confused by it really. I tried to get back. If she said, "Go and tidy your room", I'd say, "I've got to go and give someone some money." And she'd say, "I'll go and give *you* some money, if you're not careful."

'And she also used to say, "It'll be in the last place you look." Well, of course it'll be in the last place you look! You're not going to find what you're looking for and then think, "Oh, I'll just look in a few more places . . . "'

'As black as Newgate knocker'

H E Johnson of Chichester wrote: 'My late mother often used an expression which must have had very old origins. If anything was very dark or dirty – all too frequently referring to myself or my attire – she would refer to it as being, "as black as Newgate's knocker".'

Indeed, this was once quite a popular comparison, known by 1881, and alluding to Newgate gaol, the notorious prison for the City of London until 1880. It must have had a very formidable and notable knocker because not only do we have this expression but, also, a 'Newgate knocker' was the name given to a lock of hair twisted to look like a knocker.

'Good stuff for backs of westcots'

Molly St P Swords of Barton-on-Sea, Hampshire, wrote of her 'very Wessex' mother that she used to say: 'That was good stuff for backs of westcots' [waistcoats] – meaning, presumably, of material that because it was not visible did not have to be very good.

'Quiet as a bit of bread'

'My mother – born and bred a Lancastrian, but all Welsh forebears, was a belter at them,' wrote Miss L Williams of Tyldesley, Manchester. 'Although I've heard many variations of one of her remarks, I first heard in my own home the aphorism, "Poverty's no disgrace but it's a damn nuisance." [Apperson finds this in the writings of John Florio, 1591, in the form: 'Poverty is no vice but an inconvenience.']

'On hearing a friend criticized, she once said: "Not Doris, her's as quiet as a bit o' bread." When we (her five children) were mooning around, she would say: "Don't stand there like one o'clock half struck; do something."'

Partridge/*Slang* defines 'like one o'clock half-struck' as 'hesitatingly' and finds it in use by 1876.

'To take away the taste'

Victoria Glendinning, the biographer, recalled: 'My Mum – if she'd had a piece of cheese after her tea or her supper or whatever it was – would say, "I think I'll just have a little pudding to take away the cheese taste" or if she had just finished with the dessert, she would say, "I think I'll just have a little cheese to take away the sweet taste." I would wait for it and it would always come.'

'Ins and Outs of a Merryman's backside'

Rose Shipton of Stroud, Gloucestershire, wrote: 'When confronted by any complicated form to be filled in, my mother would remark that the inquirer wanted to know "the ins and outs of a Merryman's backside". This rather unrefined expression became general in the family.'

'They sticks to me heart like a glue pot!'

Jeanne Davies of Penarth, wrote: 'My mother used to greet

the family and young children with the following words: "I loves you me darlin', your eyes are like mill wheels. They sticks to me heart like a glue pot!" If anybody knows the origin of this I should be very interested to know.

'She also said to my daughter, who wanted to buy some ear-rings, "Only common girls and Catholics have their ears pierced."'

'The far end of the fart'

W G Wayman of New Barnet, Hertfordshire, remembered: 'My mother, who was born in Lincolnshire, was wont to say of a person she considered too inquisitive: "He always wants to know the far end of the fart and where the stink goes."'

Compare this from Anne Marie Hawkins, Cowbridge, South Glamorgan: 'My grandmother said of an inquisitive woman of her acquaintance: "She wanted to know the far end of a goose's trump, how many ounces it weighed, and which way the stink blew."'

'Just in time or born in the vestry'

The writer Antony Jay recalled that this is what his mother would say when arriving late. He also remembered that when she was about five she was told by a mischievous elder cousin that the cure for warts was to stand outside church on a Sunday and say, as the vicar came out, 'I wish me warts were up your bum!' It is not known how effective this is as a remedy.

'Don't do as I do, do as I say'

Margaret Martin of New Malden, Surrey, wrote: 'My mother

communicated in epigrams. As a child, how my heart sank when I heard, "Don't do as I do, do as I say" [In John Selden's *Table Talk*, 1689, on 'Preaching', he remarks, 'Preachers say, "Do as I say, not as I do".'] And "No, you can't go to the seaside – I have a bone in my leg", [This humorous excuse, sometimes '. . . in my throat/arm/etc.' goes back to the sixteenth century.] If I complained that I could not find something, I was told, "I saw the dog eating something." Needless to say, no dog!

'When trying to reinforce an argument with "so and so said", the reply (if a male was quoted) was, "Oh, he's like the barber's cat. Full of wind and water" (to rhyme with hatter) [Partridge/*Slang* has 'like the barber's cat – all wind and piss', and dates it from the late nineteenth century]; if a woman, "She says anything but her prayers." [Apperson finds 'He says anything but his prayers and then he whistles' in 1732; six years later, Swift has in *Polite Conversation*, 'Miss will say anything but her prayers, and those she whistles.']

'The *pièce de résistance* was saved for the polishing of furniture or cleaning windows. She would stand back and with a sigh of satisfaction exclaim, "There – shining like shit on a barn door!"' [Partridge/*Slang* has 'shine like a shitten barn door' and finds an allusion to the phrase in Swift's *Polite Conversation*, 1738].

As My Old Nanny Used to Say

More influential and sometimes – nay, frequently – more memorable than mothers are nannies, professional, semi-professional and honorary. The traditional British nanny is not what she was. There is certainly less of her. But the spirit of nannyism lives on in everything from Conservative women prime ministers to – very occasionally – au pairs and baby sitters. And, be she nanny, granny or 'nursey', whatever she says is never forgotten. 'All my life I seem to have been "putting myself forward", as my old nurse used to say' – so wrote James Agate in *Ego* (1935) at the age of fifty-eight.

Few professionals have built up such an array of verbal lore. Handed on from generation to generation, perhaps even taught at nanny schools nowadays, these pearls are an essential part of their technique. Two books, *The Rise and Fall of the British Nanny*, Jonathan Gathorne-Hardy (Hodder & Stoughton, 1972) and *Nanny Says*, Sir Hugh Casson and Joyce Grenfell (Dobson Books, 1972), record pages of that bossy (and, occasionally, pig-headed) wisdom. Here are just a few gems, particularly where a nannyism has entered the family mainstream:

'You'd be late for your own funeral'

'Back in the knife-box, little Miss Sharp'

Addressed to a person with a sharp tongue – compare

'You're so sharp you'll be cutting youself.' Paul Beale found a homely example of the knife-box version in Donald Davie's autobiographical study *These the Companions* (1982): 'More than twenty-five years ago I [composed] a poem which has for epigraph what I remember my mother [in Barnsley, Yorkshire] saying when I was too cocky as a child: "Mr Sharp from Sheffield, straight out of the knife-box!"' [Sheffield has for centuries been the centre of the English cutlery trade.]

'A dry bed deserves a boiled sweet'

'Fish is good for brains'

'Mr Gladstone chewed every mouthful of food thirty-two times before swallowing'

W E Gladstone, four times Liberal prime minister in the late nineteenth century, was held up as an example to countless generations of children as the man who did this tedious thing. In the BBC TV programme *As I Remember* (30 April 1967), Baroness Asquith (Lady Violet Bonham Carter) gave an eye-witness account of the Grand Old Man's jaw in action. She recalled having had a meal with Gladstone, when she was a little girl, but – horrors! – he did no such thing. Quite the reverse in fact: *he bolted his food.*

Confirmation of this deplorable fact also came in a lecture given by George Lyttelton at Hawarden (Gladstone's old home) on 24 June 1955: 'More than one lynx-eyed young spectator [has discovered] that Mr Gladstone did not chew every mouthful thirty-two times ... though I am not sure that Mr Gladstone himself might not have made some weighty and useful observations on the common and deplorable gap between principle and practice.'

'Somebody got out of bed the wrong side today'

That is, 'You are in a temper.' Why this should have anything to do with the way you got out of bed is not clear. More or less traditional: *Marvellous Love-Story* (1801) has, 'You have got up on the wrong side, this morning, George', and Henry Kingsley, *Silcote of Silcotes* (1867) has: 'Miss had got out of bed the wrong side.'

'You have made your bed and now you must eat it'

A play upon the proverb 'As you make your bed, so you must lie on it' which was known by the sixteenth century (according to the *CODP*).

'If wishes were horses, beggars would ride'

The proverb in this form was in existence by the eighteenth century (*CODP*).

'Save your breath to cool your porridge'

A proverb in similar form existed by the late sixteenth century (*ODP*).

'Think of all the poor starving people in Africa/China/India'

I had always taken this to be a (British) nanny's expression, but the nearest I can find, recorded in the Grenfell/Casson *Nanny Says* (1972), is, 'Think of all the poor starving children who'd be grateful for that nice plain bread and butter.'

Wasn't it also advised that it was polite to leave a little food on the side of the plate 'for the starving in India' if not for 'Mr/Miss Manners'?

Paul Beale in Partridge/*Catch Phrases*, commenting on the American 'Remember the starving Armenians', notes: 'The one used to exhort me as a child, late 1930s, to clear up my plate or to tackle something I found unpalatable was "Think of all the poor starving children in China!"'

As for, '...when people are starving in India...', I am indebted to *The Complete Directory to Prime Time Network TV Shows* (1981) for the information that when a proposed US series called *BAD Cars* crashed in 1980, Everett Chambers, its executive producer, said, 'We bought $40,000 worth of cars to smash up, and we never got a chance to smash them up. I think that's kind of immoral, $40,000 worth of cars to smash up when people are starving in India.'

'Cat got your tongue?'

A challenge to the mute. The *OED2*'s earliest citation is H H

Harper, *Bob Chadwick* (1911): 'I was so angry at her that I...made no answer...Presently she said, "Has the cat got your tongue?"'

'There's more ways of killing a cat than choking it with strawberries'

A variant of the proverb 'There are more ways of killing a cat than choking it with cream' (the original recorded by the mid-nineteenth century) (*CODP*).

'Cold hands warm heart'

A proverb first recorded in 1903 (*CODP*).

'The nicest things come in smallest parcels'

A version of 'The best things come in small packages', a

proverb well established by the late nineteenth century (*CODP*).

'There are three sorts of Sin – Little Ones, Bigger Ones, and Taking Off Your Shoes Without Undoing the Laces!'

A bossy injunction, quoted by Gathome-Hardy, as above.

'Queen Anne's dead'

A phrase used to put down someone who has just told you something that you know already. H L Mencken's *Dictionary of Quotations* (1942) glosses it slightly differently: 'Reply to an inquiry for news, signifying that there is none not stale.' He also supplied the alternative 'Queen Elizabeth is dead' and said that both forms appear to date from *c* 1720.

In George Colman the Younger's play *The Heir-at-Law* (1797), there occurred the line: 'Tell 'em Queen Anne's dead'. She actually died in 1714. Apperson dated 'Queen Anne is dead' to 1722, in a ballad: 'He's as dead as Queen Anne the day after she dy'd' (which doesn't seem to convey the modern meaning of the expression); and 'Queen Elizabeth is dead' to 1738 in Swift's *Polite Conversation*:

What news, Mr Neverout?

Why, Madam, Queen Elizabeth's dead.

Partridge/*Slang* also dates 'My Lord Baldwin is dead' to *c* 1670–1710. An American equivalent is 'Bryan has carried Texas' – presumably referring to William Jennings Bryan (*d* 1925) who stood three times unsuccessfully for the US presidency.

'A little older than my teeth and as old as my tongue'

What nannies should reply, when asked their age by inquisitive young persons. Jonathan Swift had it in *Polite Conversation* by 1738.

'The best doctors in the world are Doctor Diet, Doctor Quiet and Doctor Merryman'

This nannyish sentiment goes back to Jonathan Swift, according to the actor Michael York in his autobiography *Travelling Player* (1991). Nay, even further: Apperson has a citation from 1558.

Theatre people also have a similar expression that reflects rather the curative powers of getting on with the job – 'Doctor Greasepaint/Doctor Theatre will cure me.' Both versions were quoted in obituaries for the actress Irene Handl in November 1987 as being favourite phrases of hers. They not only suggest that acting is a cure for ailments, but also imply that actors *have* to be well most of the time to perform their function. The actor Bernard Bresslaw told me in 1991 that his preference was for 'Doctor Footlights will cure me.'

The creation of an imaginary doctor's name can also be found in the nickname 'Dr Brighton' for the healthy seaside resort.

'Boney will get you'

A curiously enduring threat. Although Napoleon died in 1821 (and all possibility of invasion had evaporated long before that), the threat was still being made in the early twentieth century. In 1985, the actor Sir Anthony Quayle recalled it from his youth and, in 1990, John Julius Norwich remembered the husband of his nanny (from Grantham, interestingly) saying it to him in the 1930s. He added: 'And a Mexican friend of mine told me that when she was a little girl her nanny or mother or whoever it was used to say, "*Il Drake* will get you" – and that was Sir Francis Drake!'

Ask Your Father

Fathers would seem to be a fraction less quotable than mothers and nannies. Why should this be? Discuss. The only word I have from my own father is 'fizzog'. If he was trying to wash my face when I was little, he would ask me to present my 'fizzog' to him. Not for many years did the coin drop and I realized that he was using a dated bit of slang for my 'physiognomy'. It would have helped if I could have seen the word written down – 'phisog', 'physog' or 'phyzog' make the connection more obvious. This form was recorded first in 1811, but other abbreviations (phiz/phizz/phyz) go back much further.

My father would also say, 'No, thank you, I have had an excellent sufficiency' when declining an offer of more food. Paul Beale's *Concise Dictionary of Slang*...(1989) has this, rather, as 'an *elegant* sufficiency...Jocular indication, mocking lower-middle-class gentility, that one has had enough to eat or drink, as "I've had an elegant sufficiency, ta!" since *c* 1950.'

Other fathers have said this sort of thing:

'But you don't look it'

Mary Collins from Cowbridge, South Glamorgan, said that her father, on meeting one of the opposite sex for the first time, would invariably inform her: 'I don't know your age, madam, but you don't look it.' Mrs Collins added that every woman took it as a compliment.

'After all, none of us is human'

Julie N Hynds of Uxbridge, Middlesex, wrote: 'My father's favourite is "After all, none of us is human." He didn't invent this, but its origins are lost in the mists of time.'

'Never wrestle with a chimney sweep'

From the *Observer* Magazine (4 July 1993) on Tony Benn MP: 'Now he is older he finds himself repeating advice his father offered him as a child like "Never wrestle with a chimney sweep", which means don't soil yourself by responding to your opponents' dirty tricks. "The whole wisdom of humanity is summed up in these phrases," he muses.'

'I see you're unpacking your trunk'

Bill Shuard of Portrush, County Antrim, remembered: 'My father had an admonition that I have never forgotten. If he saw any of us young children picking our noses he would say, "You're staying then? I see you're unpacking your trunk."'

'There, that'll stop you farting in church'

Jim Diston of Minehead, Somerset: 'This was the family saying that was invariably used by my father when he was obliged to act in order to prevent us youngsters from meddling with anything dangerous or from straying beyond control. He would place something beyond our reach or lock it away. He would say it to his ducks and chickens, too – and to himself when he considered that he had put right someone who had chanced their arm with him.'

Partridge/*Catch Phrases* suggests that a politer form of this remark was 'That will stop him laughing in church' and that the original 'That will teach him to fart in chapel/stop their farting in chapel' (ie 'that'll stop them from taking liberties') is possibly an English public school expression of the 1930s.

'Tomorrow will be Friday'

Joan Bell of Cambus, Clackmannanshire, recalled: 'If as a child, disappointed over something, I gave a wail of "Ooh!", my father would join in with, "Ooh! Tomorrow will be Friday and we've caught no fish today." I don't know the origin of this, but I think it must be a song of the Edwardian era. Comic opera perhaps? Is there one about monks?'

Well, there is a painting by Walter Dudley Sadler entitled *Thursday*, which is also known as *Tomorrow Will Be Friday*, so perhaps that's it.

'Makes old men young, young men strong'

A Lancastrian saying, used when recommending food, by the father of Joan Bakewell, the broadcaster. He would also encourage his children to eat up quickly by urging, 'Them as finished first can help the others...'

'Strong enough to trot a mouse on'

'My father, who was in the army for much of his life, always enjoyed a cup of tea but didn't like it too strong. If it was, he would remark that it was...' – J G Hills of Bitterne, Southampton.

'I am, by the way, always intrigued by a phrase which I seem to have picked up for use when some unexpected mishap nearly arises. On such an occasion, one feels obliged to say, "Whoops, Jemima!" But who was Jemima in the first place?'

Ah, a good question. Since the nineteenth century, the name 'Jemima' has been applied to 1. any servant girl 2. a chamber-pot. I don't think we need to look too far to find a situation in which 'Whoops, Jemima!' might have been spoken.

'Charm the bird from the tree'

Writer and journalist Celia Haddon quoted a saying of her father's in the form of 'Darby Haddon's Law': 'Never build a house, breed a horse or keep a woman. You'll always find someone else to do it for you.' Also, as he was a farmer, when things went badly, he was wont to say, 'Well, if you put your hand into the hand of God Almighty, you must expect a rough ride.'

And his advice to his female children about how to get their own way was: 'Charm the bird from the tree. Don't throw a bloody great brick at it.'

'Dover's on the lee bow'

Francis Matthews, the actor, recalled that although his father was not a naval man, he would wake his children up by brushing back the curtains and saying, 'Wakey wakey, rise and shine, the sun's burning your eyeballs out and Dover's on the lee bow!' He was actually 'Indian army', so he would also say "*Jildi kerau!* [hurry up, immediately]'.

'The filthy Prussian habit . . .'

A N Wilson discovered when he was writing a biography of Hilaire Belloc that, for the last ten years of his life, Belloc seemed like an automaton – he always repeated the same old things. If anybody put a plate of mutton with redcurrant jelly in front of him, he would always say: 'Ah, the filthy Prussian habit of eating jam with meat.' And when he was driven to London from Sussex past a certain house, he would point it out to his children, and say, 'That is the house of George Meredith – or, as some say, Me*re*dith – who thought in Welsh to his dying day and was always so kind to your dear mother.'

'I lift up my finger and I say "tweet-tweet"'

Bryan Magee, the philosopher and broadcaster, remembered that when, as a little boy, he wanted to do something and went to ask his father if he could, his father would say, 'I lift up my finger and I say "tweet-tweet"' – 'and that meant I couldn't do it.'

The song whose title line this is was written by Leslie Sarony in 1929.

Magee's father also used to say, 'The proof of the pudding

is in the lap of the gods.' 'I think it was a line from a play he'd seen with Mrs Patrick Campbell. We always used to say it when anything was uncertain.'

'You got up before you went anywhere...'

Keith Wilyman of Horton, Northampton, wrote: 'If being made to jump by someone appearing suddenly and unexpectedly, my late father would say, "God – you might as well kill a man as frighten him to death!" And if you met him earlier than arranged, his remark was always, "*You* got up before you went anywhere this morning!"'

'As the monkey said...'

The (Irish) father of the singer/songwriter Dillie Keane apparently always says, when speaking to her over the phone, 'Ah, you're looking well.' And, 'if as a child, you said you couldn't wait for something, he would repeat: "As the monkey said when the train ran over its tail, 'It won't be long now.'"'

This last, according to Partridge/*Slang*, is but one of the

'As the monkey said' remarks where there is always a simple pun at stake: eg '"They're off!" shrieked the monkey, as he slid down the razor blade.'

'You've been a bit early of late'

Ray Parkerson of Letchworth, Hertfordshire: 'I should like to share with you a saying of my late father's, which was sometime before the Second World War. He would often come out with, "You've been a bit early of late, you used to be behind before, but now you're first at last." No explanation was ever given for this, so I assume it was a compliment from one person to another on timekeeping.'

'Times is hard'

Suzanne King of Hyndland, Glasgow: 'For years, as we sat down to tuck into our Christmas lunch, my father would say, "Times is hard." Now he doesn't have to say it, we just say, "Yes, Dad!"

'My grandfather always says of people who can't make up their minds, "He doesn't know whether to shit or light a fire." Apparently this refers to soldiers who, at the end of a long day's march can't decide whether to warm up first, or...'

'Breakfast is a farce'

Anne Tayler of Nazeing, Essex: 'My father always used to say this. As a child I had no idea what he meant. I think he meant it was a silly or unnecessary meal.

'My grandfather, who I am glad I didn't know, had two

sayings that outlived him. One was, "Everybody is wanted but nobody is wanted much." And the other was, "Do I want it? Yes. Do I need it? Yes. Can I live without it? Yes."'

'You're big enough and ugly enough'

In her book *Daddy, We Hardly Knew You* (1989), Germaine Greer described how she had researched her father's true history to find out the answers to questions about him that had always tantalized her. Along the way, she recorded Reg Greer's way of putting down children's questions. 'At the dinner-table where we children were forbidden to speak,' she wrote, 'he occasionally held forth ... [but] if I pounced on some statement that seemed to me to reflect however dimly upon the real world [he would say], "I've forgotten more than you're ever likely to know."' Greer commented: 'This fatuous hyperbole dismayed me ... but perhaps after all it was literally true. Daddy's whole life was an exercise in forgetting.' Another put-down, 'You're big enough and ugly enough to take care of yourself.' And, for twenty years, if asked, 'What's the time?', he would invariably reply, 'Must be. Look how dark it is.'

Germaine Greer also recalled: 'There was an elaborate family word-play on the phrase "Tosti partood" (the *tood* to rhyme with *wood*) which I realized many years later was an encoded memory of Tosti's "Farewell".' [Italian-born Paolo Tosti (1846–1916) was appointed singing master to British royalty in 1880, took English nationality and was knighted. His song 'Good-bye' was very popular.]

'You'd disgrace a field of tinkers'

Journalist John Walsh described how his father, a West Coast

Irishman, would say this of John's attempts to grow his hair long in the 1960s.

'Let's run down to the store and stock up before the hoarders get there'

The crime writer Paula Gosling was brought up in Detroit. This is what her father would cry whenever they were running out of any household supplies.

'Halt! The dust-brown ranks stood fast'

The writer and actor Patrick Barlow described his father as a completely unliterary man but this did not stop the father from ritually reciting a line from Virgil's *Aeneid* whenever he met anyone who vaguely hinted at a classical education – '*Incipiam. Fracti bello fatisque repulsi...*' [Bk II, line 13]. But, chiefly, whenever the Barlow family motor reached and stopped at a halt sign, Barlow *père* would *always* declaim a 'line from Ella Wheeler Wilcox': 'Halt! The dust-brown ranks stood fast.' Sometimes, however, this was abbreviated to 'Halt, the dust-brown.'

In fact, the line comes rather from John Greenleaf Whittier's poem 'Barbara Frietchie' (1863) which celebrates the old lady who waved a Union flag at Stonewall Jackson's troops as they passed through Frederick, Maryland, during the American Civil War. This is the poem that includes the immortal couplet:

'Shoot, if you must, this old gray head,
But spare your country's flag,' she said.

Mr Barlow's cherished line comes just before this:

Up the street came the rebel tread,
Stonewall Jackson riding ahead.

Under his slouched hat left and right
He glanced; the old flag met his sight.

'Halt!' – the dust-brown ranks stood fast.
'Fire!' – out blazed the rifle-blast.

We'll All Sit Down Together

The actor Peter Jones said of his American mother-in-law that she was 'a very good cook and hostess, and used to make marvellous meals, but she didn't much enjoy clearing up afterwards. So she used to say, "We'll all work together and then we'll all sit down together." It's an awfully good recipe and my wife and I carry it on at home.' Here then are the sayings which may involve all – or any member – of the family.

It is odd how many have to do with food. Hence the common initial instruction 'F H B' ('Family Hold Back'), meaning that certain food in short supply is not to be eaten by members of the family when guests are present (and mentioned in Ian Hay's *Safety Match*, 1911) – also 'F H O' ('Family Hold Off') and 'F K O' ('Family Keep Off'). As for 'T T T' ('Tummy Touching Table') – this was either a parental instruction not to eat too much or an indication that one could not eat any more. 'M I K' meant 'More In the Kitchen', in other words, 'Go ahead and eat it' (Partridge/*Slang* has this by 1939).

'He won't be called Clarence any more . . . '

Enid Grattan Guinness of Bengeo, Hertfordshire: 'Always quoted when a fly was killed or, later on, whenever anybody got killed in a radio or TV programme: "He won't be called Clarence any more . . . " I think it came from a melodrama my parents saw in their courting days in the very early 30s, possibly at the New Cross Empire.'

Betty Burke of Trowbridge, Wiltshire came up with a possible source. She remembered from her schooldays an example in an English grammar book ('probably illustrating the accusative case') – 'They used to call him Clarence, but they call him nowt now, for I murdered him last Monday.'

Poor Clarence, whichever one he was! He had an interesting death, of course, and not with a fly-swat, in Shakespeare's *Richard III*. Partridge/*Slang* remarks of the name: 'Like, though less than, Cuthbert, apt to be used as a jocular colloquialism.' Paul Beale added: 'A *Punch* cartoon of 2 February 1916 may be relevant; it shows an officer and a sergeant discussing a distant sentry: *Officer.* "Why do you think he wouldn't make a good corporal?" *Sergeant (indicating sentry).* "'I'm a corporal! Lor Lumme! Why, 'is name's Clarence!"'

'The hour of the tea cosy is past'

From L B Pulsford of Cambridge: 'This is a family saying of ours which is still in use after more than a hundred years. My grandmother was engaged to be married in the 1870s. Shortly before the wedding, an elderly lady friend of the family told her that she had a wedding present for her – a tea cosy – if she would call on a certain day and collect it. My grandmother forgot, and went a few days late, with many apologies, but was met by a stony-faced lady who said, icily: "The hour of the tea cosy is past", and shut the door.'

'True, O King!'

When I have made an obvious statement, perhaps even a pompous one, my wife has a way of saying to me, 'True, O King!' I wondered where she had picked this up from until one day I happened to see some old film of Charles Laughton indulging in a spot of public reading from the Bible, as he was latterly wont to do. He was telling the story of Nebuchadnezzar and the gentlemen who were cast into the burning fiery furnace, from Daniel 3:24. Nebuchadnezzar asks, 'Did not we cast three men bound into the midst of fire?' – 'They answered and said unto the king, True, O king.' So that was it.

The nearest Shakespeare gets is the ironical '"True"? O God!' in *Much Ado About Nothing* (IV.i.68), though he has any number of near misses like "True, my liege', 'Too true, my lord' and 'True, noble prince'.

Just to show that my wife is not alone – Mrs H Joan Langdale of Tunbridge Wells wrote to me and said, 'My father, a Classical Scholar and an Anglican priest, used to use your wife's quotation "True, O King!" and always added, "Live for ever."'

'You won't feel the benefit of it'

Brian Cooke of Cheltenham, Gloucestershire, remembered:

'When someone called during the colder months of the year and seemed likely to stay for more than a few minutes, it was customary to say, "Won't you take off your coat? Or you won't feel the benefit of it when you go out."' Compare these words of wisdom from the family of Derek Robinson, the writer: what to say about clothing when the weather's bad: 'If you've got it, you can always put it on, but if you haven't got it, you can't take it off.'

'And I always get the tip-up seat'

From Jenny Searle of Welwyn Garden City, Hertfordshire: 'One quote from *Much Binding in the Marsh* has become a family catchphrase ever since childhood. Sam Costa, feeling hard done by, would go into an inaudible muttering session, finishing with "And I always get the tip-up seat." This is used by anyone who thinks they're being put upon.'

'See who's given up smoking'

I Moore of Manchester wrote: 'My father was the youngest of a large family and when his older sisters used to read the deaths in the paper, they used to say, "I'll just see who's given up smoking." For years, he used to think that if you gave up smoking, your name went in the newspaper.'

'Nice dinner – for a change'

C J Misselbrook of London SE6 wrote: 'When I was a lad, my family regularly ate Sunday lunch together – that lunch consisting of the traditional "roast and two veg". On one particular Sunday, however, my mother produced a different main course – possibly steak and kidney pie. Having finished and obviously thoroughly enjoyed the meal, my aunt put down her knife and fork, sighed and said, "Nice dinner for a change." Now, if any out-of-the-ordinary meal is served, someone in the family is bound to say, "Nice dinner – for a change."'

'That's the last time you have Ribena in the drawing-room'

'The children, now in their forties, insist that it was Mother who spilt it. Be that as it may, the saying is still in regular use to mark any domestic mishap' – M G L Foster, Yeovil.

'A long thing and a thank you'

'We say this to any elongated article, I've no idea why,' wrote Marie Brazier of Potters Bar, Hertfordshire. 'As a child, I spent holidays with my parents in Dover. It was often cold and windy and I used to grumble, shivering, "rotten old Dover". Now, cold windy weather in our family is "rotten old Dover". A cousin wrote to me recently, "plenty of rotten old Dover this year".

'My aunt was giving tea to some nieces and as they were quite young she made it weak and milky. She asked, "Do you have tea at home, Lily?" Lily replied, "Sometimes we have tea and sometimes we have this." Now if a cup of tea turns out weak we say, "Hmm, sometimes we have this."'

'Yum, yum, pig's bum!'

A commonly known way of expressing that food is delicious. The actor Robin Bailey remembered it as a 'Black Country' saying, in the form 'Our mam, pig's bum'. The actress Helen Atkinson Wood coupled it with two other rhyming lines: 'Liar, liar, pants on fire' and 'Super dooper, Gary Cooper'.

'Perfectly nice'

Isabel Colegate, the novelist, remarked that the trouble with family sayings was that, very often, you didn't notice them yourself. 'I remember a few years ago being very surprised when somebody laughed at us for using the phrase "perfectly nice" when we actually mean the opposite. You meet someone and the others ask what were they like and you say, "perfectly nice" – and you mean "so boring that it's not worth my bother trying to describe it to you". And in the same way, you might be going out and you'd come in and say, "Do I look all right? Is this dress all right?" And if they said, "That looks perfectly nice", you'd go straight upstairs, probably in tears, and change everything...'

'Wireless ear'ole'

Just after the First World War, Alan E Peters, later of Bexhill-on-Sea, lived in South London with his parents: 'At the time, hearing aids were somewhat bulky and primitive, and consisted of a battery-box and microphone worn on the chest, with a wire leading up to a headset rather like the old headphones we used to listen to the early radios.

'Our neighbour was a London taxi-driver who was the archetypal cheerful Cockney character. One day he was describing to my Father an acquaintance that for the moment my Father could not recall. The taxi-driver tried all ways to jog my Father's memory, until finally in desperation he said, "You must know 'im, Arfur, 'e's a big tall fella wiv a wireless ear'ole."

'From them on, of course, within the family, hearing aids were always referred to as "wireless ear'oles". Even years later, when my Mother had to take a hearing aid, she would refer to it as her "wireless ear'ole".'

'It's a first-class thing'

In *Conversations with Max* (1960), S N Behrman recorded this from the writer Sir Max Beerbohm: 'Let me tell you about a phrase that was current in our family... It came from Johnston Forbes-Robertson. He was somewhere... and he noticed a mezzotint of some eighteenth-century admiral that hung on the wall. He reflected how dreary it was. Mrs Patrick Campbell sailed in. Her eye went at once to the admiral. She began rhapsodizing about him; she became aerated about that admiral – to the delight of the host, of course, who hadn't realized he had such a masterpiece on his wall. Mrs Campbell couldn't say enough about the mezzotint – it made the room, it transported you. When she had done, she swept down on Johnston. "Don't you agree?" she demanded. Johnston was determined to puncture the tyre of Mrs Campbell's ecstasy. "Yes," he said calmly, "it's a first-class thing." We never stopped using it. When I was drama critic on *The Saturday Review* and came back to

Upper Berkeley Street after a play and my mother asked me about it, that phrase would save me more ample criticism.'

'The peacocks are lovely and they're low down on the ground'

Claire Hawthorn of Norwich wrote: 'We had just descended from the top of Warwick Castle, down a steep, spiral staircase. At the bottom were two couples discussing whether they would make the ascent. One of the women said plaintively, "The peacocks are lovely and they're low down on the ground." This is now our family saying for getting out of difficult activities.'

'Doing a Gore'

In the family of Duff and Lady Diana Cooper – at least according to their son, John Julius Norwich – this was the expression for 'doing something that you did not want to do, in order to be polite to somebody else who didn't want to do it either'. For example, 'doing a Gore' was if you were invited to Christmas lunch with some people and did not want to go but went anyway. Who 'Gore' was remains a mystery.

'Wouldn't I jist, Mum!'

Dorothea Jamieson of Devizes, Wiltshire: 'We have two expressions which have become adopted by the family. Just after the First World War when 'flu and consumption were rife – neighbours of my mother were afflicted and a girl from the country came to Southsea to help their household. My grandmother was rather sorry for this Winnie and asked her to tea. As she ate, she belched and said, "Manners! – I always sez that when I does that."

'And the second? My mother as a smallish girl was reading *Punch* and this joke caught her attention: the picture was of a little waif looking through the railing at children in a garden. A lady stopped and said, "Would you like to be playing with those children?" – Child, "Wouldn't I jist, Mum!"

'My mother and I continued to use these expressions till the end of her life.'

'Through leaves'

Vita Sackville-West, the novelist and poet who was married to Harold Nicolson, explained a family expression of hers in a broadcast talk called 'Personal Pleasures' during 1950: 'They rustle, they brustle, they crackle, and if you can crush beech nuts under foot at the same time, so much the better. But beech nuts aren't essential. The essential is that you should tramp through very dry, very crisp, brown leaves – a thick drift of them in the autumn woods, shuffling through them, kicking them up ... walking in fact "through leaves".'

Hence, the family phrase to express pure happiness of the sort enjoyed by young children shuffling through drifts of dry autumn leaves. It spread, at least as far as James Lees-Milne, later to become Harold Nicolson's biographer. In a diary entry for 9 January 1949, he wrote: 'I made a little more progress with my book this weekend, but no "through leaves" as I should like. Laboured, factual and stodgy stuff churned itself out' (*Midway on the Waves*, 1985) .

The Nicolson/Sackville-West family had several phrases. Nigel Nicolson in a note to *Harold Nicolson Diaries and*

Letters 1930–1939 (1966), comments on their now notorious word 'bedint': 'It comes from the German *bedienen*, to serve, and "bedints", in Sackville language, originally meant "servants". But "bedint" also meant "vulgar" or "genteel" or "lacking in standards".'

'Who's a clever Chibiabos, then?'

Gerry Lakin of Whitfield, Dover: 'When I was evacuated during the last war, the elderly lady of the house in Ashby-de-la-Zouch where I was billeted, would say when any of her charges got above himself, "Who's a clever Chibiabos, then?" Chibiabos was a friend of Hiawatha [and an admired musician] in Longfellow's poem.'

'Could I press you to a jelly?'

'I had an uncle who used to amuse my little friends at tea parties by saying he was so hungry he could "eat the dates off a calendar". He called my mother's fancy cakes "ooja-ka-pivs" for want of a special name and would say such things as "Can I press you to a jelly?" which made the small guests collapse in mirth' – Helen Rudge, Sway, Hampshire.

'Throwing it around like snuff at a wake'

'My elderly Irish aunt used to say this about people who were overly generous with their money' – Marie Hartshorne, Shaftesbury, Dorset.

'Neither arse nor elbow'

Doris Humphrey of Grantham wrote: 'I had an aunt who had an apt and witty saying for every eventuality – sometimes rather sharp and not very kind, but always apt.

'Of anyone she knew who had got above themselves, she would say, "The peas have grown above the sticks."

'Of a married woman who was known to be having a bit on the side: "A slice off a cut loaf is never missed" [Shakespeare has an earlier version of this proverb in *Titus Andronicus*, 1592].

'Of any rather odd looking married couple: "As He makes them, so He matches them."

'Anything doubtful was "Neither arse nor elbow" – the meaning of which defeats me!

'Finally, one from my father: "Trust in the Lord, and keep your bowels open."'

'Angels moving their beds'

From Ken Marshall of Basingstoke, Hampshire: 'The uncle and aunt who raised me in the 1920s taught me about thunder: "Don't be afraid – it's only the angels moving their beds."'

'It is better to have your tail pulled than to be ignored'

R J Watkins of Marske-By-Sea, Cleveland: 'This was a saying often heard in our house. It could be attributed, if he could have talked, to an affectionate but eccentric cat we once had.'

'Sit on your grand-dad's grave and have a rock-bun'

'I know these are not brilliant,' said Glenys Hopkins of Warrington, Cheshire, 'but they are genuine Family Sayings rather than catchphrases or ancient/local slang. In the days before theme parks and garden centres, when it was quite usual to go for a Sunday picnic which included a visit to the family grave, a child in the party fell over and was comforted as above. This phrase has been used ever since in our family as slightly mocking comfort, particularly if someone has been making an inordinate fuss about some minor mishap.

'On another occasion, one of my mother's cousins was being teased about her latest young man, who was, in today's terms, rather a wally. She defended him as follows: "He's got a kind heart, even if he does wear woolly gloves." This phrase has come in very useful ever since to identify without condemning anyone with wallyish tendencies.'

'May you do so mightily!'

Robert Clayton of Cardiff: 'My father loved reading, particularly non-fiction, and when I was a schoolboy in Beaumaris, Anglesey, in the 1950s, he read a book about a primitive tribe living in the jungles of South America. They would gather round the camp fire and, when one of them wished to visit the toilet, he would stand up and announce his intention to the whole assembly, which would then chorus, "May you do so mightily!" On his or her return from the jungle, they would announce, "I have done so mightily!"

'This became the norm in our family for many years – you can imagine the effect on friends who came to visit . . .'

'That is what the soldier said'

Dorothy M Wolfe of Clarks Summit, Pennsylvania, inquired about this phrase. She did know the similar 'That is what the girl said' but with 'at the picnic' added. These are probably earlier versions of the more recent 'as/like the man said' or 'as the girl said to the sailor' which are both used as throw-away, humorous tags, though not quite to the subversive extent of 'as the bishop said to the actress'. Partridge/*Catch Phrases* suggests that the origin is the passage from Charles Dickens, *The Pickwick Papers* (1835–7) where Sam Weller remarks during the trial of Mr Pickwick, 'Oh, quite enough to get, Sir, as the soldier said ven they ordered him three hundred and fifty lashes' and the judge interposes with, 'You must not tell us what the soldier, or any other man, said, Sir. . . it's not evidence.'

'Off we go and the colour's pink'

In 1980, Anthony Smith of Pinner, Middlesex queried the origin of this phrase which he said was used when re-starting some social activity/topic of conversation/fresh round of drinks. Many years later, Donald Hickling of Northampton commented: 'I heard this catchphrase in "Metroland" (to the north of Pinner and slightly to the left) in a respectable hostelry one Saturday lunchtime when the host or master of ceremonies, a WW2 naval officer, was remembering how a liberal supply of pink gins kept him going, and he assumed that everyone in his company appreciated "pinkers". And, in the context of family sayings, I can quote the parent of a friend who was wont to exclaim, "Up she goes and her knickers are pink." Metroland again!'

'Why keep a cow when you can buy a bottle of milk?'

A common justification for not getting married. Hence, the comic confusion of this version: 'Why go out for a pint of milk when you've got an old cow at home?' Partridge/*Slang* also finds this 'cynical male gibe at marriage' in the forms 'Why buy a book when you can join a library?' and 'You don't have to buy a cow merely because you are fond of milk', dating them from the late nineteenth century. He also suggests that the 'milk/cow' argument features in John Bunyan's *The Life and Death of Mr Badman* (1680), though this has not been verified and is probably not used in connection with marriage. Apperson also finds the simple expression 'Who would keep a cow when he may have a quart of milk for a penny?' by 1659.

'Captain Pumpernickel of the Swiss Navy at your service, ma'am'

Anna Briggs of Cullercoats, North Shields, said that in her (Canadian) husband's family this was a standard self-introduction. Sounds a touch Marx Brothers, does it not?

'Farewell, baskets, the grapes are gathered'

Peter Jones's Uncle Harry used to come out with this quotation, as a way of ending something. It puzzled Peter until a listener to *Quote... Unquote* supplied the information that it was from *Gargantua* by Rabelais – in French, *'Adieu paniers, vendanges sont faictes.'* A friar, Jean des Entommeurs, is exhorting his fellow monks to stop praying and repel the soldiers who are vandalizing their vineyard. A call to arms.

'It's enough to make a parson swear'

Colleen Spittles of Deal, Kent, remembered members of her family saying this after any form of aggravation. Indeed, it is a well known expression and quite old. Edward Ward used it in *Hudibras Redivivus* (1706): 'Your Folly makes me stare;/Such talk would make a Parson swear.'

'Moaning Minnie'

Norman Beaumont of Ropley, Hampshire, wrote: 'I was born in 1941. If I had the grizzles as a toddler, I used to be told, "You are a moaning minnie."' Indeed, like so many alliterative phrases this has had considerable staying power. Anyone who complains is a 'moaner' and a 'minnie' can mean a lost lamb which finds itself an adoptive mother. But the original 'Moaning Minnie' was something quite different. In the First World War, a 'Minnie' was the slang name for a German *minenwerfer*, a trench mortar or the shell that came from it, making a distinctive moaning noise. In the Second World War, the name was also applied to air-raid sirens which made that sort of sound. Subsequently the term was applied to people rather than things. On 11 September 1985, Margaret Thatcher paid a visit to Tyneside and was reported as accusing those who complained about the effects of unemployment, of being 'Moaning Minnies'. In the ensuing uproar, a Downing Street spokesman had to point out that it was the reporters attempting to question her, rather than the unemployed, on whom Mrs Thatcher bestowed the title.

Another example, from the *Observer* (20 May 1989): 'Broadcasters are right to complain about the restrictions placed on them for the broadcasting of the House of Commons ... But the Moaning Minnies have only themselves to blame.'

Mr Beaumont also remembered people saying in the 1940s, when 'sitting down to eat rationbook food at home, "That's the stuff to give the troops".' Partridge/*Slang* actually dates this from the First World War but defines it simply as 'That's the idea, that's what we want', and not necessarily about food.

Mr Beaumont continued: 'The third phrase was "Before the war!" This I heard daily at home, during and after the [Second World] War as a hark back to better times. I still use this now, imitating my parents, and bringing up a loud groan from my own children.'

'If that's your best, it's rotten!'

The lawyer Helena Kennedy, QC, was brought up in a Scottish Catholic household. 'We frequently used to say, "Pray to Saint Anthony" – that was because if anything was lost, apparently Saint Anthony was the man to recover it for you. But the favourite thing that was always repeated in our house were my granny's dying words. She was very ill and the doctor would come to see her. And she would say, "How am I doing, doctor?" and he'd pat her on the hands and say, "I'm doing my best, Mrs Jones." And she said to him, finally, "If that's your best, it's rotten!" And so frequently in our household if people say, "I'm doing my best", we all say, "Well, it's rotten!"'

'It comes more of a beige, Modom'

Paul Beale, reviser of Partridge/*Catch Phrases* and Partridge/*Slang*, remembered: 'In my own family, sayings were mostly quotations from genteel shop assistants as above (I grew up in Tunbridge Wells). At the end of a long order to the grocer (in the days when customers gave orders in shops), he would inquire, "And would there be anythink more besides?"

'Eavesdroppings on the bus, late 1940s, that lingered: one woman telling another how much she had enjoyed seeing the film "the Force it sayga"; and another, on her medical history, in a loud voice, "It's not the womb, ducks – it's me choobs." Several other sayings, as is probably so in many families, are private and perhaps rather cruel jokes against members of the family for some lapse in manners, taste or unselfishness.

'My wife's family, however, had a nice one that alluded back to an early C20 dialogue that is supposed to have taken place between her maternal grandfather, who was a master cabinet-maker in North Finchley, and one of his craftsmen:

Grandfather: Is that job finished yet?

Craftsman: It's near enough.

Grandfather: Near enough's not good enough. It's got to be just right.

Craftsman: Well, now, it *is* just right!
Grandfather: That's near enough then.

'So now, two generations later, "That's near enough" covers the whole thing. Actually, although the family was convinced of its authenticity, it has the look of one of those long drawn out late C19 *Punch* captions.'

'Too late! Too late! the Captain cried, and shook his wooden leg'

Stephen Ingle of Dartford recalled this phrase 'In memory of my mother-in-law', though he did not make it clear whether this was something she herself used to say or whether there was some other connection. Compare what Partridge/*Catch Phrases* calls originally a military catchphrase – 'Too late! too late!' spoken in a high falsetto, after the story of 'that luckless fellow who lost his manhood in a shark-infested sea very soon after he had summoned help'.

T A Dyer of London SW12 noted that his father used to say (in the 1940s):

'"It's come too late!" the lady cried, as she waved her wooden leg – and passed out.'

In c 1984, an American professor queried the saying, '"Aha!" cried she, as she waved her wooden leg, and died' – which is clearly related. Donald Hickling of Northampton recalled a nonsense poem that his father brought back from the First World War which included the phrase, 'Waving her wooden leg in dire despair'. He added that his family would exclaim it whenever a disaster-prone neighbour hammered on the party wall.

Possibly connected, John Gray of Sutton wanted to know the source and correct form of a couplet that his father used to quote at him when he was a boy:

**'Too late, too late, shall be the cry
When you see — passing by'**

Sir David Hunt suggested that this was probably a corruption of a hymn to be found in the Sankey and Moody hymnal. Indeed, the final couplet of the concluding verse of 'Jesus of Nazareth passeth by' by Miss Etta Campbell and T E Perkins is:

**'Too late! too late!' will be the cry –
'Jesus of Nazareth *has passed by.*'**

This came as a revelation to Stuart Holm of Norwich who recalled living in Morecambe when he was a student at Lancaster University in the late 1960s. 'A regular Sunday ritual was a stroll along the promenade with a few fellow students. Among the delights on offer, a street trader was usually to be found selling a variety of wares to the accompaniment of the inevitable sales patter. He adapted "too late, too late" as part of his sales pitch, leading on one memorable occasion to the unforgettable phrase, "Too late, too late will be the cry, when the man with the gents fully automatic umbrella passes you by." Umbrella was pronounced "umbarella" and the overall effect so amused my friend Ross Reynolds and I that it became a catchphrase for the rest of our time at university.'

Llywela V Harris of St Davids, Dyfed, remembered from her childhood the pithier 'Too late, too late, the pawnshop's shut!'

'Fish knives an' all!'

Margaret Hines of Lymington, Hampshire, wrote: 'My Granny was staying to look after the family while my Mother was confined for my birth. She had cooked fish for lunch and asked the cleaning lady to lay the tray for the patient. "Where are the fish-knives?" demanded the charlady. Granny replied that we had none and ordinary knives would do. The job was completed in tightlipped silence. When she presented the tray to my mother, the charlady announced, "My sister's got a lovely house in Bedford. Fish-knives an' all!" Mother was somewhat puzzled by this until Granny related the earlier conversation and for ever afterwards we used "Fish-knives an' all!" to describe superior people.'

'Have plenty of vegetables ... '

'Before the war, my late father, being of a kindly disposition, used to visit a number of pensioners in a row of almshouses,' said David Hine of Temple, Buckinghamshire. 'To his surprise, one of the old ladies invited him to lunch. He duly attended and, as they sat down, she said, "Now, Sir, have plenty of vegetables ... the meat cost sixpence."

'This became a family joke and, with wartime rationing, often did much to cheer a meal when in fact the meat was often non-existent – or cost less than ninepence.'

'Thank God and the good British Navy for our food'

Kathleen Kent of Caton, Lancaster, offered: 'A saying which, I imagine, was unique to our family. At the dinner table, we children (all five of us) would chant this "grace before meat", with folded hands. The period? First World War. My father? A sailor.'

'Life is hard'

This stern text was always quoted to Peter Wood, the theatre director, by what he called his West Country 'Protestant Work Ethic' family. Many years later, he was struggling upstairs with his parrot, Sid, in his cage – when the parrot, too, suddenly said it to him.

Other forms of this exclamation would include the tradition: 'It's a hard life', 'Life is hell', 'Life is not a bed of roses', 'Life wasn't meant to be easy', 'Life is unfair'.

'It do, don't it'

Daphne Ibbott of Hereford: 'In the 1920s, my grandparents took a lodger from Norfolk whose favourite expression was "It *do*, don't it?" One year, our family took a holiday in Cromer and, on arrival, mother made a remark about the weather to our landlady, who replied: "It *don't*, do it?" This riposte has lived on in our family.'

'Work hard, play hard, Xenophon was a Greek. Use your toothbrush daily. Hack no furniture'

According to the writer Gemma O'Connor, this curious set of admonitions was embroidered on a cushion cover in the house of the publisher Sir Rupert Hart-Davis. What had Xenophon to do with any of it? Well, a number of *Quote...Unquote* listeners recognized the phrases as coming from those 'copy books' that schoolchildren once used to practise their handwriting. These consisted of lines of printed copperplate writing interspersed with blank lines for the child to write on. One correspondent remembered them from her own schooldays *c* 1925 and said the books were still in print in 1948. Another noted: 'The phrases were quite random – chosen, I imagine, to fit the space available and/or to give the child the opportunity of practising different combinations of letters... The compiler must have had quite a sense of humour to juxtapose such phrases – it certainly amused my husband (who was born in 1917) or he would hardly have remembered it from his early childhood.'

Incidentally, Gemma O'Connor said that when she does something particularly nice for her husband, John, he says: 'That was A and B the C of D' (Above and Beyond the Call of Duty). And that John's (Irish) father – who had nine children – was wont to remark, 'Many are called, but few get up.'

'Thumthing from the big thity'

Liz Lochhead, the poet and playwright, said her family sayings were full of charm to her because they were largely incomprehensible. 'No one could get on a bus without saying what apparently one of my Aunty Agnes's boyfriends had once said. If we were going on a bus to Glasgow which was only twenty miles away: "Can I bring you back thumthing from the big thity?" (it always had to be done with a lisp).

'And, also, no one in our family has ever been able to refuse a cake or a biscuit without quoting one of my Aunt Elsie's boyfriends: "Oh, no thanks, any more would sicken me."'

'As queer as Dick's hatband'

Tony Brisby of Little Haywood, Staffordshire, recalled: 'A sentence used by my grandmother was, "He's as queer as Dick's hatband – it went round twice and then didn't meet." I have absolutely no idea what she meant.' Marjorie M Rawicz of Sandiacre, Nottinghamshire, recalled: 'As a young person in the Twenties, I remember my Mother (Derbyshire with Yorkshire roots) saying "You're as funny as Dick's hat band" when either my sister or I was being contrary and difficult. I heard no more of this expression until the late Sixties when a Miss Emily White (from Cheshire) told me that *her* Mother finished the quote –

"Funny as Dick's hat band – it went twice round and then would not tie".'

David Scott of Windermere recalled his grandmother saying in the 1930s – if things didn't work out: 'That's like Dick's hatband – it went round twice and still didn't fit!' Dorothy Hoyle of Grantham added that, in her family, it was always 'as *black* as Dick's hatband' when something was very dirty. Mrs J M H Wright of Ilkley countered with: 'The correct version – "as *near* as Dick's hatband" – makes the saying self-explanatory, at least to a Yorkshire person. "Near" in Yorkshire speech as well as meaning "close to" also means "mean or stingy with money". Thus the person referred to is as "near" with money as Dick's hatband is "near" to Dick's head.'

So, lots of variations. The *OED2* gives the phrase thus: 'as queer (tight, odd, etc) as Dick's (or Nick's) hatband', and adds: 'Dick or Nick was probably some local character or half-wit, whose droll sayings were repeated.' Partridge/*Slang* describes it as 'an intensive tag of chameleonic sense and problematic origin'. He dates the phrase from the mid-eighteenth to the early nineteenth century, finds a Cheshire phrase 'all my eye and Dick's hatband', and also a version that went, 'as queer as Dick's hatband, that went nine times round and wouldn't meet'. In Grose's *Dictionary of the Vulgar Tongue* (1796), Partridge found the definition: 'I am as queer as Dick's hatband; that is, out of spirits, or don't know what ails me.' A 'Newcastle form *c* 1850' is the 'nine times round and wouldn't meet', just given.

But who was Dick, if anybody? *Brewer's Dictionary of Phrase and Fable* is confident that it knows the answer: Richard Cromwell (1626–1712), who succeeded Oliver, his father, as Lord Protector in 1658 and did not make a very good job of it. Hence, Brewer believes, 'Dick's hatband' was his 'crown', as in the following expressions: *Dick's hatband was made of sand* ('his regal honours were a "rope of sand"'), *as queer as Dick's hatband* ('few things have been more ridiculous than the exaltation and abdication of Oliver's son') and *as tight as Dick's hatband* ('the crown was too tight for him to wear with safety').

Compare what Harry Richardson of Virginia Water, Surrey, said *his* grandmother (1870–1956) used to say in answer to a child's curiosity: '"You are as queer as a Norwegian fiddle"... I saw the artefact many years later. It has two frets!'

'Well, she certainly fell with her bottom in the butter'

The writer Mark Steyn's mother is Belgian and, so he said, is 'not very good at proverbs in English but uses a lot of Belgian expressions'. This is what she said 'when my third cousin eight times removed got married'.

'Keeping B and S Tog'

Joan Bell of Cambus, Clackmannanshire, remembered: 'In my late husband's family, a great saying when serving up a substantial snack or full meal was, "There you are, that will keep B and S Tog" [Body and Soul together].'

'Keeping body [or life] and soul together' is, of course, an old phrase. According to the *OED2*, 'Tate' in Dryden's *Juvenal* (1697) has: 'The Vascons once with Man's Flesh (as 'tis sed)/Kept Life and Soul together'. Jane Collier, *The Art of Tormenting* (1753) has: 'By never letting him see you swallow half enough to keep body and soul together.' *The Century Illustrated Monthly Magazine* (November 1884) has: 'How on earth they managed to keep body and soul together.'

'I'm not having this...'

Sheila Hancock, actress, who is married to John Thaw, actor, admitted to the family saying, 'I'm not having this – I'm off, mate!' Apparently it came from what the comedian Max Wall told John Thaw had been said when he was appearing in a terrible pantomime with 'Monsewer' Eddie Gray. Wall and Gray were playing the King and Queen of Hearts. 'It was one of those shows with a pop star as Dick Whittington, tatty costumes, and the stage machinery was clanking behind them. Not to mention an indifferent audience. Suddenly, Eddie Gray turned to Max Wall and said "I'm not having this – I'm off, mate!" . . . and walked out, removed his makeup and drove back to London!'

'And all's yet unachieved!'

Thelma Pearce of London SW 17 revealed: 'In our house, when we are running late and all the clocks strike, this cry goes up. "Where's that from?" I asked my husband recently. He confidently plumped for *The Lady's Not For Burning*. But I said, no, *The Love of Four Colonels*. Turned out I was right. Is it vintage Ustinov or was he quoting too?'

'Your mum should have tucked your ears in'

A W E Hellingman of Overton-on-Dee, Clwyd, wrote: 'It is curious how often it is that the better off people seem to get the majority of windfalls such as legacies, Premium Bond wins and the like, whereas those who would appreciate a little help never seem to strike it lucky. An expression used by my parents whenever they heard of such an event was, "The devil always shits on the biggest heap" – which I believe originated in Holland.

'Also, as a little boy in Holland, I used to go to school in winter wearing a beret. My Mother always used to pull it down over the tips of my ears, whereas other children used to arrive at the school presenting a decidedly goofy appearance with their ears doubled over or sticking out sideways. The expression therefore evolved in our household that whenever anyone did anything silly or careless, "Your mum should have tucked your ears in" or "It's the way your mum put your hat on."'

'Do you come from Bardney?'

Steve Race, the musician and broadcaster, wrote: 'Small boys brought up in the city of Lincoln, as I was, will testify that if one left a door open, someone would be sure to say, "Do you come from Bardney?" Bardney is nine miles south-east of Lincoln and there was formerly an Abbey there, presumably with an "ever-open door".' Apperson finds this expression being discussed in *Notes and Queries* by 1905.

'And what's the drink situation?'

Anthony Thwaite, the poet and literary editor, recognized that in his household this was a phrase always used prior to a dinner party. So much so that when his daughter Alice was aged about five and was asked what she had learned at Sunday School, she replied – apropos the water-into-wine miracle at Cana – that she had been told about 'Jesus and the drink situation'.

'We're in God's Pocket, living up here'

Mrs V Evrington of Ynysddu, Gwent, wrote: 'While living

further up the valley in an area with a lovely view, my family used to say this.'

'Sugging'

Once when I was appearing in 'Dictionary Corner' on Channel 4's *Countdown*, I introduced this new seven-letter word (not yet in any dictionary). I had been told of its existence by someone involved in market research. It refers to the very irritating practice of people who pretend to be carrying out an opinion poll but are really trying to sell you something. In other words, they 'S U G' – 'Sell Under the Guise' (of market research).

I thought it was a word – or, rather, a meaning of a word – that deserved to have a wider audience, but, as you might guess, 'sugging' has long existed in other fields. Literally fields, actually. 'Sugging' is an adjective meaning 'soaking' and has been in the language since the eighteenth century.

Then a *Countdown* viewer, Mrs M K Price of Filton, Bristol, wrote to inform me of yet another meaning, hitherto known only to her nearest and dearest: 'In our family *sugging* has been a word for nearly thirty years. "To sugg" is to take forty winks; "sugging" is indulging in forty winks; and "feeling sugnacious" is to desire forty winks. My airline pilot son introduced the word to his fraternity, and someone came up with "suggery", the indecent act of dozing off on the job, such as when driving.

'It all started when the family cat was sitting bolt upright, swaying, with her eyes like two bright slits. A very young grand-daughter pointed at the cat and, screwing up her eyes, said, "Cindy sugg", meaning "shut". Being a daft lot, it caught on.'

'Even digging ditches is some lot easier than having to work with people'

Vernon Rogers of Bath wrote to say that he came originally from near Land's End where, because unemployment was always a fact of life, the family traditionally had to leave home to seek employment. 'As a result of so many of us doing quite a range of jobs in so many parts of the world, we agree on one thing – our family saying.' Mr Rogers also pointed out that 'some lot' is a West Cornwall expression.

'Sky-blue scarlet...'

Mrs J Jones of Shrewsbury recalled: 'As a small child, when I asked an Aunt what was the colour of something, she would teasingly reply, "Sky-blue scarlet, the colour of a mouse's fart" – to the annoyance of other adults. I have never heard this from anyone else, and have no idea whether or not it was my Aunt's original.'

Well, Partridge/*Slang* has 'sky-blue pink' for 'colour unknown or indeterminate', since *c* 1885.

'I've got a touch of the Buddy Grecos'

Chrissy Blake of London W4 wrote: 'Sitting watching Buddy Greco on TV in the early Sixties with my sister (we were both teenagers), we both felt sick at the same time and vomited before going to bed. Ever since, if feeling sick, members of our family say, "I've got a touch of the Buddy Grecos".'

'And when it stops ... '

Judith Smith of Felthorpe, Norwich, recalled an interesting family use of a stock phrase from BBC Radio's *Listen With Mother* broadcasts for small children. Apart from 'Are you sitting comfortably? Then I'll begin', another familiar phrase from the programme was when the story-teller would say, 'And when the music stops, Daphne Oxenford [or A N Other] will be here to tell you a story...' Judith Smith felt sure, however, that the phrase was, rather, '...and when it stops...': 'Our surname being *Stopps*, my late husband always vowed that if we had a son he should be called "Wennit". Fortunately, perhaps, we only had daughters.'

'Botty with drawers on'

From Jennifer Forsyth of Grange-over-Sands: 'A family expression, now being used by the fourth generation, often startles the uninitiated. My mother's eldest sister, born in 1897, had been asked out to tea by a neighbour and she was to go there unescorted. This caused her some anxiety and she asked her mother, "What shall I say when I get there?" The reply didn't allay her fears and she kept on repeating, "But what shall I say...?" Her youngest sister was quite exasperated by all this shilly-shallying and crossly retorted – "Oh, say 'Botty with drawers on'" – the rudest thing she could dream up in 1905. Since then, if there is nothing to be said, it is "B W D O", which might be received on a postcard from foreign climes, or as a response to routine family inquiries on health or the state of the nation.'

'Life is real, life is earnest...'

John G Dudderidge of Luton proffered a Dudderidge family saying when someone is complaining about something: 'Life is real, life is earnest and the grave is not the *gaol.*' Mr Dudderidge added: 'Presumably *gaol* for *goal*, but origin unknown.' I think I can help him there. Try Longfellow's 'A Psalm of Life' (1838):

> Tell me not in mournful numbers,
> Life is but an empty dream!
> For the soul is dead that slumbers,
> And things are not what they seem.
> Life is real! Life is earnest!
> And the grave is not the goal;
> Dust thou art, to dust returnest,
> Was not spoken of the soul.

Also from Mr Dudderidge – 'Harassed maiden aunt of my mother's (*circa* 1920) herding children in the street...a string of commands ending in "...and pull up your socks and get out of the way of the motor car" – since used to terminate any string of commands. And, on considering whether to accept a treat, "Oh well, it's the last Tuesday [or whatever] of the week..."'

'Everything's done in my own little way/My own little tea-set, my own little tray'

Barbara Wild of Rye, East Sussex, asked about this couplet –

'which has rung round our house for years. Edward Lear perhaps? It is completely evocative of a certain type of person – our type, I fear.' It remains untraced.

'More tea, vicar?'

A correspondent who, understandably, wished to remain anonymous advanced this family phrase, 'for after a fart, or to cover any kind of embarrassment'. Paul Beale has collected various forms for a revision of Partridge/*Catch Phrases*, including: 'good evening, vicar!'; 'no swearing, please, vicar' (said facetiously to introduce a note of the mock-highbrow into a conversation full of expletives); 'another cucumber sandwich, vicar' (after an involuntary belch); 'speak up, Padre!/Brown/Ginger (you're through)' (as a response to a fart).

The writer Andrew Davies was quite open in referring to his mother-in-law's expression after a fart: 'Oh, it's just a little wee one in its stockinged feet.'

'Mind you, I'd never *harm* a cat'

Andrew Davies also mentioned of this same mother-in-law that she had a way of qualifying her remarks. She would come out with things like: 'I've always preferred dogs. I've never been fond of cats – mind you, I'd never *harm* a cat.' And Andrew says the family has found this a useful formula.

They are not alone. Doris Herbert of Lymington pointed out that in Hugh Walpole's novel *The Cathedral* (1922), there occurs this passage: 'The Archdeacon looking at them from his stall, could not but feel that they were rather a poor lot. Not that he exactly despised them; he felt kindly towards them and would have done no single one of them an injury.'

Household Names

A subdivision of household catchphrase-making is the bestowal of names on household objects. Quite why people do this, I don't really know. Or perhaps it is that they just say they do in order to make excruciating puns.

In May 1986, a BBC Radio 4 programme called *English Now* attracted claims of the following domestic nomenclature:

a house called 'Lautrec' because it had two loos;

a car called 'Simon' because it had a rattle;

a Hoover called 'J Edgar';

a car called 'Flattery' because 'it would get you anywhere'

– and so on . . .

Best of all, at round about the same time, a viewer of Channel 4's *Countdown* wrote to tell me that he had a wok called 'Hereward'. Michael Rosen, the poet, told me – on a related theme – that his mother used to refer to the dishwasher as a 'wish-dasher' which, as he sagely points out, would be a useful name for almost any household goods.

In *Conducted Tour* (1981) Bernard Levin recounted of Sir Michael Tippett, the composer, that, a good many years ago, he had used the fee paid to him by a television company for an interview, to buy a washing machine. According to Levin, he felt it was only right to name the device after the benefactor who was, at least, indirectly responsible for his being able to afford it. 'Hence, the odd but pleasing fact – pleasing to me, anyway, that there is a washing-machine in Wiltshire called "Bernard Levin".'

House names themselves have frequently been bad-punned. I might mention, apart from the obvious 'Dunroamin', 'Dunbankin' and so on, some other sightings (and citings) including: 'Copper Leaves' (the home of a retired policeman), 'Aftermath' (retired maths teacher), 'Stumps' (dentist), 'Bedside Manor' (doctor). Make what you will of: 'Suitsus', 'Kumincyde' and 'Thisledoo'. (Acknowledgements to Leslie Dunkling, author of *The Guinness Book of Names*, 1974, for these last few.)

And today we have naming of pets . . . Interesting names are similarly sometimes bestowed on household pets, especially cats:

'Pardon and Toilet' – by students of U and Non-U language, presumably;

'Castor and Pollux' – but the owners only ever called out by name for Castor;

'Derry' – an unneutered female. This enabled the following explanation of why she was mating: 'Oh, it's just Derry and Toms.'

'Keith and Prowse' – because they always got the best seats in the house.

'Ceremony' – belonging to a woman who had to warn visitors not to stand on it.

'Chew and Lie' – Siamese kittens, one greedy, the other always sleeping.

''Er Outdoors' – by contrast with the expression ''Er indoors' (meaning 'the wife', unseen, but domineering), as popularized by George Cole as Arthur Daley in the ITV series *Minder* (from 1979).

In 1973, I ventured inside the household of Peter Spence, the TV scriptwriter, and discovered that the dog was called 'Woolworths' and the cat 'Boots'. James Morris in *Pax Britannica* (1968) recounted how when the Prince of Wales returned from a visit to India in 1876, he brought with him two tigers named 'Moody' and 'Sankey'. More recently, I have heard of a pet tarantula called 'Sting'.

Grandmother's Footnotes

Deaf people have discovered, willy-nilly, the art of putting a spoke in conversations from which they may rudely have been excluded. My maternal Grandma was a past mistress at this sort of thing. She wore a hearing aid – somewhere about the size of Jodrell Bank or Goonhilly Down – which was pinned to the front of her capacious bosom. To relocate this instrument she would turn her bosom in the direction from which she supposed sound was coming. She would then turn up the volume so that all sorts of howls and whines were emitted. After a while, Grandma would invariably give up the attempt, turn off the machine and lapse into brooding silence. Then she would plot how to disrupt our activities.

Her finest moment came once when we were sitting round the tea-table, debating the great issues of the day, and, as usual, excluding the poor old thing from our conversation. Suddenly, she erupted with the startling inquiry: 'How's your telephone, Bill?' It took us only a moment or two to realize that not one of us round the tea-table was called 'Bill'. More slowly, it dawned that Grandma had embarked on one of her many pet theories, that she was being over-charged for her telephone calls. From that day on, in our family, the phrase 'How's your telephone, Bill?' has been ritually employed whenever anybody has wanted to change the subject. Or to bring a conversation to a juddering halt.

(Someone not from our family once told me that their deaf granny had come up with the equally efficacious 'But wasn't he a Smith-Bosanquet?' – which had a similarly emasculating effect on conversation.)

Here now are the sayings of some other fondly remembered – or otherwise – grandmothers, together with a few from grandfathers who, on this showing, are less likely still to be quoted these days:

'Why bother? – no one is going to stop a galloping horse to look at you!'

'When we looked in the mirror or took trouble with make-up, my grandmother would make this remark,' said Miss K E Bagley of Dursley, Gloucestershire. 'And if family arrangements were altered and she was told about it, she would say: "Oh, well ... anything for a change – as the old woman said when she kissed her cow."'

'Like a Drury Lane fairy'

Violet Mills of Cuckfield, West Sussex: 'I'm 70 years old and was brought up by a grandmother who in turn was brought

up by a mother who took in washing at the back of Leicester Square. When I came home crying because I'd fallen over and hurt myself, my grandmother always said, "You're like a Drury Lane fairy – always in trouble." She would never tell me what a Drury Lane fairy was...'

Understandably. J Redding Ware's *Passing English of the Victorian Era* (1909) defines a 'fairy' as 'a debauched, hideous old woman, especially when drunk'. Francis Grose's *Dictionary of the Vulgar Tongue* (1785) has 'Drury Lane vestal' = 'harlot'.

'The man on the beach with a worsted nose'

George Goldsmith-Carter of Walmer, Kent, wrote: 'When I was young, eighty years ago, I lived with my grandmother on the Suffolk coast at Aldeburgh. When I did anything silly or inept she would say, "You are like the man on the beach with a worsted nose who has never seen the sea." When I was doing something and making a mess of it, her son Harry (my favourite uncle and a yacht skipper) would say to her, "You are making a real Margaret Hakon of that boy." Whoever was Margaret Hakon?

'Whenever I made an extravagant or boastful utterance, my grandmother would say, "Yes, yes, I've heard geese fart before in windy weather." Once when I was helping a fisherman haul a boat up a steep shingle beach and was all out of breath, he said to me: "Easy boy, George, easy... there's a difference between having a good shit and tearing your arse."'

'There are no pockets in shrouds'

Ena Constable of London N20: 'My grandfather believed money was for hoarding, not spending. When budget discussions were about to become arguments, my grandmother would look him straight in the eye and with total conviction say, "George, there are no pockets in shrouds." This saying has become a household word.'

R C Trench, *On Lessons in Proverbs* (1854) refers to an Italian proverb, 'With an image Dantesque in its vigour, that "a man shall carry nothing away with him when he dieth", take this Italian, *Our last robe...* is made *without pockets.*' In English nowadays, this proverb Is more usually: 'Shrouds have no pockets.'

'You have to eat a peck of dirt before you die'

Alison Vallins of Arundel recalled: 'When we were children and fussy with our food, my grandmother used to say: "Don't worry. You have to eat a peck of dirt before you die."'

She was not alone in this. This proverbial saying is quite widespread, though Apperson first finds it in 1639 in the form, 'You must eat a peck of *ashes* ere you die.'

'He's like Joe Soap – he has to put a potato in the window to know what day it is'

Said by the grandfather of Chris Kelly, the broadcaster. Also – of a stupid person – 'If all the hairs on his head were drumsticks, there still wouldn't be enough to beat them out.'

'Till the rooks...'

'Our family saying is used rather like "And pigs might fly" in reply to anyone wondering aloud. It originated with my grandmother who died in 1933. To children endlessly speculating about anything, she would flatly admonish them with: "You'll wonder till the rooks build in your backside – and then you'll wonder where the sticks came from!"' – Mary Smith, New Romney, Kent.

'Money – and fair words'

The actress Diana Quick said that her grandmother (clearly an honorary nanny) came from Suffolk. When asked how much anything cost, she would reply, 'Money – and fair words.' She would also observe, 'The only place success comes before work is in the dictionary.' Diana's (Irish) mother-in-law, Kate, had a nannyish phrase, too. If people were getting above themselves and boastful, she would say: 'I saw a shabby funeral. They need a trumpeter.' This echoes the old saying, addressed to an egotist, 'Your trumpeter is dead', which Apperson finds by 1729. From Baker's *Northamptonshire Glossary* (1854): 'Sometime it is said [again to an egotist], "Your trumpeter's dead", ie no one sounds your praises, so you are compelled to extol yourself.'

'Fat sorrow's better than lean'

Donald Rimes of Ashford, Middlesex, wrote: 'A Londoner myself, I was intrigued by this phrase used by my wife's Yorkshire grandmother.' As well he might be.

"Owt to come, glad of it'

'Whenever anyone offers me anything, or asks if I could make use of this or that, I offer them this family saying: "Like me granny said to the bookie, "'Owt to come, glad of it'." I am 65 and remember her saying it to the bookie's runner when he used to call at the house for her daily threepence each way' – Ron Farley, Selby, North Yorkshire.

'Ah, well, I'm off to have a bath in a teacup'

Mrs Anne Hill of Innsworth, Gloucestershire, remembered that this is what her Gran would say as she went off to bed. 'When you realize she was a dumpy little woman who wore long dresses and looked as if she moved on castors, you can imagine what a lovely picture it conjured up.'

'There's just enough for tomorrow'

The South-African-born broadcaster Sue MacGregor had a Scottish granny with a habit of serving roast chicken – 'the fowl' – at Sunday lunch. When there was not quite enough to go round, her phrase was: 'Would you like some more, dear?...because if you wouldn't, there's just enough for tomorrow.'

'What a world it is for woossit...'

Mrs F Smith of Adel, Leeds, wrote: 'I had a country-bred Grandmother and her sayings are now part of family lore. My own grandchildren hear me using them, so the phrases go on in time: "God does not take given flesh." "Walking about to save funeral expenses." "The little white hen who never laid away." (About a baby:) "His heart's asleep."

'And, especially, "What a world it is for woossit, and nobody knows how to knit" (and all are baffled by the word "woossit").'

Vera Geddis of Eastleigh, Hampshire, misheard this last as 'What a world this is for *worsted*' and was reminded of a saying of her mother's: 'What a world this is for worsted, fourteen balls of cotton for a penny!' She added: 'I cannot recall my mother ever explaining her saying – I am not certain whether the number of balls was fourteen or sixteen – but I assume that the point of it was that when tempted to bewail the state of the world, one cheered oneself up by changing it into a statement about the amazing cheapness of worsted.' Indeed, Wright's *English Dialect Dictionary* (c 1900) gives 'worset' as a form of 'worsted', so there seems to be more than the glimmer of an explanation here.

'You must wear clean underwear in case you get run over'

Jean Boht, the actress, recalled advice that has been given to many a young person – in her case, from her grandmother, in the form: 'Always wear a clean pair of knickers, dear, in case you get run over.' 'And she also used to say, "If you think you're in love, just think of him sitting on the lavatory. If you still love him, marry him."'

'Give it all up, dear, and come home'

Humphrey Carpenter, the biographer, recalled something that his grandmother, an almost-literally Victorian lady, used to say. She had four beefy, energetic daughters and, if they complained about what happened when they went out into the world, she would say: 'Give it all up, dear, and come home.' As a result they never did (come home). Humphrey added: 'When my own children show signs of wilting – or I do – I say the same.'

'There never were such times since Old Leather Arse died!'

Jean Ford of Red Cow Village, Exeter, wrote: 'When Grandma was alive, she would say this on auspicious occasions. As we all thought it rather rude, this later became "Never were such times . . . you know, since when!" No idea who Old Leather Arse was.'

Roger Traill of Highcliffe-on-Sea subsequently recalled the version used by his grandfather, E W Westbrook (1877–1956): 'There never were such times since old Leather-arse fell out of the brake and busted the beano.' Mr Traill thought this must refer to an annual works outing of some kind (beano) by coach (brake): 'I suspect that the manager or some other member of the office staff would have been the natural target of such ribaldry. This is further reinforced by the definition of "leather-bottom" ("a Civil

Servant tied to his desk") and "shiny-bum" ("to have a desk-job") in Eric Partridge's slang dictionary.'

Mr Traill's grandfather spent most of his life in and around London's East End and evidently had quite a fund of jocular expressions: when confronted with an obvious exaggeration or lie, he would say: '... and the band played "Believe it if you like..."' Referring to any impish rascal or mischievous child: 'He's a red-nosed robber' (could this have anything to do with 'the red-nosed rooter', a naval port-maintopman, as mentioned in John Masefield, *The Conway*, 1933?) When asked if he knew a particular person: 'Oh, yes. He used to chew bread for our ducks.' His name for Adolf Hitler or other prominent Nazi: 'Herr-Trigger Back-Stud.' When meeting an acquaintance unexpectedly or in passing: 'I can't stop, I'm waiting for somebody!' Apropos nothing in particular: 'Who put pepper in the cat's milk?' When trying not to swear: 'Hearthstone, brick dust and ruddy whitening.' (Hearthstone was a name for butter, so is this instead of 'bugger'?)

Mr Traill added that his late grandmother, Ellen Elizabeth Westbrook, in a similar predicament, would exclaim something to the effect: 'Tooka-marka-booka-shooka-Annie.'

Compare, from A E McLachlan of Cirencester, Gloucestershire: 'This saying came to me, via my mother, from a great-uncle. The man had never been known to swear, but to vent his feelings he would say, "Jam butter and plaster the dandelion, old bucket!"'

And from Mrs E Vera Rich of London E4: 'My maternal grandfather who died in the 1920s was a staunch Methodist, so he would not swear. Instead, according to my mother, he would say, "XYZ TEAPOT AND H FOR RESURRECTION!"'

'I never heard him say it, but I did often hear him say, "Short and sweet like a roast maggot."'

'Every little helps – as the old lady said when she piddled into the sea'

'My old Gran used to say it,' remembered Jack O'Farrell of Billingham. In fact, lots of people did/do. It is a pretty common saying of the 'Wellerism' type.

'Caught in my disbil'

June Hennessy of Lohitzun Oyhercq, France, wrote: 'Whenever my grandmother opened the door to an unexpected visitor before she was properly dressed (but without a hair out of place), she always complained of being "caught in my disbil". It wasn't until I came to live in France that I realised she must have anglicised the word *déshabillé...*'

'A1 at Lloyds, B2 at Osbornes'

The grandmother of Charles Osborne, the Australian-born writer, was a Lloyd before she married into the Osbornes. She had nothing to do with Lloyds in the insurance sense but she evidently found plenty of opportunity to go round the house saying this to the annoyance of her husband.

'Sometimes I just sits and thinks and sometimes I just sits'

Until recently this well known saying did not feature in any dictionary of quotations. On first being asked about it, people would invariably say, 'Oh, that's what my grandfather used to say.' So where did it originate? In the novel *Anne of the Island*

(1915) by L M Montgomery, the Canadian writer who had earlier written *Anne of Green Gables*, an old woman who drives a mail-cart remarks: 'O' course it's tejus [tedious]. Part of the time I sits and thinks and the rest I jest sits.' Was this the first outing for what was clearly to become a much used and popular saying? No, it was not.

On 24 October 1906, *Punch* carried a cartoon which showed a vicar's wife talking to an old, somewhat rustic, gentleman who has been laid up with an injured foot. She is sympathizing with him and saying: 'Now that you can't get about, and are not able to read, how do you manage to occupy the time?' He replies: 'Well, mum, sometimes I sits and thinks and then again I just sits.' Headed, 'Change of Occupation', the cartoon was by Gunning-King.

'And your friends will like you'

Bryan Magee, the philosopher and broadcaster, recalled that when his grandfather was offered something with the words, 'Help yourself', he would reply softly: 'And your friends will like you.' This I take to be based on the Scottish proverb, 'Help thyself, and God will help thee', which has been known since the eighteenth century.

'Like Launceston gaol'

John A Hill of London SWI: 'My Westcountryman grandfather, describing an untidy scene, would say that it looked "like Launceston gaol". Pronounced "Lansen" by him, the gaol had none of the renown of Princetown Prison not far away on Dartmoor. How, then, did a little town's lockup become a byword for disorder?'

'Hang the expense and give the cat another kipper'

Jane Klemz of Ripon, North Yorkshire, said: 'My grandfather would say this if he or anyone else was contemplating a mild extravagance. And whenever we had baked onions – which he adored – he would say: "On Stanley, on. If I stood where Stanley stood it would be On-I-On." So onions were known as On Stanleys.'

'You're like a wooden man made of smoke'

'As a young child in the 1950s, I can remember my grandfather saying this when either my brother or myself was not being very successful in our attempts to do something' – Judith Hughes of Preston.

'Stupid bird, goose – too much for one and not enough for two'

The grandfather of Antony Jay, the writer,would always say this whenever goose was served.

Tony Jay also admitted to one of his own sayings, related

to his punctu-holicism. He said he actually gets physically ill if he feels he is going to be late for something. And when he feels this coming on, he notices that one of his children will say: 'Darling, shall I ring them and say we are going to be late?' Apparently it was 'a refrain throughout their childhood'.

Knickers on the Line

Some domestic catchphrases are so widely used that it would be inappropriate to attach them to particular families. In our household, when someone asks, 'What's the time?' and the answer happens to be (as it does, frequently, for some reason), 'Half past nine', the first person says, 'Knickers on the line.' One of a number of ritual additions, this was imported by my wife from her Buckinghamshire childhood in the 1950s. In a section called 'Crooked Answers' in *The Lore and Language of Schoolchildren* (1959), Iona and Peter Opie print two versions of a rhyme from Alton, Hampshire:

> What's the time?
> Half past nine
> Put the napkins on the line.
> When they're dry
> Bring them in
> And don't forget the safety pin.

And:

> What's the time?
> Half past nine
> Hang your breeches on the line.
> When the copper
> Comes along
> Pull them off and put them on.

Now here is a small selection of similar phrases, including

some whose meaning and provenance present a bit of a problem:

'All gong and no dinner'

What you would say of a loud-mouthed person, somewhat short on achievement. On *Quote... Unquote* in 1985, Anne Diamond, the TV presenter, said she had heard it in her father's family. Partridge/*Slang* has a citation from *The Archers* in 1981.

'All round and about like Pouncer's dog'

Meaning, 'everywhere'. Told to me on an LBC radio phone-in, London, in June 1990, but otherwise untraced and unconfirmed.

'Almost good enough to eat'

A simple compliment when something (*not* food) looks attractive. Sir David Attenborough was once on a ship ploughing its way through the South China Seas and being

served with the worst food he has ever tasted in his life: 'There was a Cockney steward and when you got up every morning for breakfast, you'd go down to the cabin and the ship would be rolling around, and he'd plonk this thing down in front of you which looked absolutely disgusting, and every morning without fail, this steward would say, "There you are! That looks almost good enough to eat!"'

'Anne Gallus not wearing a tie'

Meaning, 'untidy' – specifically not wearing a tie. Told to me on that same LBC radio phone-in, London, in June 1990, but otherwise untraced and unconfirmed.

'As long as you've got your health, that's the main thing'

A conversational cliche, together with its corollary, 'If you haven't got your health, you haven't got anything.'

'As near as damn is to swearing'

Meaning, 'too close to call', or 'no difference'. I first heard it from an optician in Liverpool in 1963.

'Bless his little cotton socks!'

A pleasant remark to make about a child. As 'bless your little cotton socks', it just means 'thank you'. Partridge/*Slang* dates it from the turn of the last century and labels it heavily 'middle-class'.

'Bob's your uncle!'

Meaning 'And there you are/there you have it!'/'All will be well'/'It's as simple as that' – an almost meaningless expression of the type that takes hold from time to time. It was current by the 1880s but doesn't appear to be of any hard and fast origin. Basically a British expression – and somewhat baffling to Americans. There is the story of one such who went into a London shop, had it said to him, and exclaimed, 'But how did you know? – I *do* have an Uncle Bob!"

In 1886, Arthur Balfour was appointed Chief Secretary for Ireland by his uncle, Robert Arthur Talbot Gascoyne-Cecil, 3rd Marquis of Salisbury, the prime minister. Is that where the phrase came from, as some people fervently believe?

Miss M L King of London SW3 wrote: 'Whenever anyone says it, I reply, "And Fanny's your aunt" – I don't know why.'

'Crawly-crawly bum-lick'

Meaning 'obsequious'. Heard in 1986.

'A fit of the pearlies'

I do not know what this means but I was asked about it in 1987. A musician had said something to the effect that playing parts of Ravel's 'Bolero' was likely to bring on a 'fit of the pearlies'. One might have expected 'pearlies' to be rhyming slang, but for what? Pearly Gates/hates? Or perhaps pearlies are teeth, so it was music to set your teeth on edge? Alternatively, something to do with showing off. It is all very baffling.

'Happy birthday to Pooh/Stick your head down the loo'

Said by child at London Zoo party to mark the 60th anniversary of the publication of A A Milne's *Winnie-the-Pooh*. Reported in *New Society* (October 1986).

'Hard in, soft out'

A slogan of the Campaign for Real Bread. I was interviewing a spokesman for the campaign on the BBC Radio *Today* programme on 19 December 1977 and commented that the brown rolls he had brought along with him were, well, a bit hard. This was his reply.

'He can leave his boots/shoes under my bed anytime'

= 'I find him sexually attractive.' This was said to me by a small lady of Iranian extraction regarding Robert Redford (in April 1970). As far as I know, she still hasn't even met him.

'He is so mean he can peel an orange in his pocket'

For some reason, I have a note of this expression as having being said by a 'Welsh woman 1920s/30s'.

'I couldn't fancy him if his arse was decked with diamonds'

Ditto.

'I don't mind if you burn'

Once this was the 'smart' rejoinder to the query, 'Do you mind if I smoke?' Another form was 'I don't care if you burst into flame.' The mother of the poet Michael Rosen would reply, nudgingly, 'Before, during or after?'

'If it *looks* good, then it probably *is* good'

A curiously depressing observation. I remember hearing some desk-bound BBC wallah passing judgement on the Concorde supersonic airliner in c 1970: 'Well, what I say is, if it looks good ... '

'If it was raining palaces I'd end up with a toilet at the bottom of the garden'

The kind of thing said by the terminally miserable/ unfortunate/disaster-prone. Myfanwy Talog quoted it on *Quote...Unquote* in 1983. Compare the Australian: 'If it was raining palaces, I'd be hit on the head with the handle of a dunny [privy] door'; 'If it was raining pea soup, I'd only have a fork'; 'If it was raining virgins, I'd end up with a poofter'.

'I'm all behind like the cow's tail'

What people, like my wife, say when they are behind with their tasks. 'C H Rolph' wrote in *London Particulars* (1980): 'Grandma Hewitt [his grandmother] was a walking repository, rather than a dictionary, of clichés and catch-phrases; and I have often wished she could have been known to Mr Eric Partridge during the compilation of his delectable dictionaries. Both she and I...could pre-date many of [his] attributions. Here are four examples...all of which were common currency in my Edwardian childhood: "Just what the doctor ordered", "Are you kidding?", "Cheats never prosper", and "All behind like a cow's tail".'

'In Johnny Gough's garden'

Meaning, 'in the cemetery' = 'dead'. Told to me on an LBC radio phone-in, London, in June 1990, but otherwise untraced and unconfirmed.

'It shone like a tanner on a sweep's arse'

Peter Foulds of Darlington, County Durham, wrote: 'A Cockney cousin of mine once told me of her pleasure at receiving, from her husband, the gift of a baby grand piano. She described the beautiful lustre of the instrument with these words.' Partridge/*Slang* has 'shine like a shilling up a sweep's arse' – which is a touch more alliterative – and dates it 'early C20'.

'It's just a way of getting you through the day'

I was interviewing Frank Muir on the BBC Radio programme *Stop Press* in 1985 about his penchant for writing letters to *The Times*. This was his reply to my question as to why he did it. I don't know that it is really a catchphrase but it sounds as if it ought to be.

'It's the sign of a hard winter when the hay runs after the horse'

A proverbial expression of desperation. Or, possibly, a once-only utterance. From Arnold Bennett, *The Journals* (1971): 'Thursday, 10 August [1899] – I have just remembered a saying of Mrs Drummer, our new housekeeper at Witley. She said to me: "There's a lot of old maids in the village, sir, as wants men. There was three of 'em after a curate as we had here, a very nice young gentleman he was, sir. No matter how often the church was opened those women would be there, sir, even if it was five times a day. It's a sign of a hard winter, sir, when the hay begins to run after the horse.'

'I was born in nineteen hundred and frozen to death'

A slightly facetious way of drawing attention to one's age. Macdonald Hobley said it on BBC Radio 2 *Where Were You in '62?* in 1982. Compare, 'Nineteen hundred and mind your own business.'

'I wasn't born yesterday, you know'

Meaning, 'I'm no innocent.' The *OED2* has this as an established saying by 1757. But I can't help feeling its modern use must have been encouraged by the play/film title *Born*

Yesterday, Garson Kanin's excellent vehicle for Judy Holliday (1946), about an ignorant girl who wins out in the end.

'Larovers for meddlers and crutches for lame ducks'

This is a way of not giving an answer to an inquisitive person, especially a child. If someone asks, 'What have you got there?' this is the reply with which to fob them off. Possibly a northern dialect expression originally, but now quite widespread. Could 'meddlers' be 'medlars' (ie the fruit – also a term for the female genitals, as it happens)?

Philip N Wicks of Wellingborough, Northamptonshire, recalled: 'When as a small child I asked my Mother [who hailed from Norfolk], "What's in there?" regarding the contents of any unreadable packet or blank blue grocer's bag, she would reply secretively, "Leerooks for meddlers and beans for gooses eyes." I've wondered for forty years what she meant.'

Partridge/*Catch Phrases* finds a version already in use by 1668. Apperson explained 'larovers' as 'lay-overs' – things laid over, covered up, to protect them from meddlers – and concluded: 'Almost every county has its variation probably of this phrase. The most common form in which it survives, however, is "Layers for meddler".'

Another explanation is that 'lay-holes for medlars' are what you put the fruit in to ripen. Partridge also gives the variant: 'Crutches for meddlers and legs for lame ducks'. No easy solution to this one.

'Like a bit of egg on a shovel'

Harry Richardson of Virginia Water, Surrey, remembered: 'One of my staff, a lady particularly pleased with her salary rise, once described me thus. A Midlands expression she said!'

'Lovely weather for ducks!'

What you say when it is raining. Although it must be ancient, I have not found a citation in this precise form before 1985. However, Apperson finds 'Another fine week for the ducks' in Charles Dickens, *The Old Curiosity Shop* (1840) and suggests that the predominant form is 'Fine weather for ducks'.

'A moment on your lips, a lifetime on your hips'

A dieter's slogan. Recorded in November 1987, but much older?

'Neat but not gaudy – like a bull's arse tied up with a bicycle chain'

Told to me by an anonymous correspondent from the Cotswolds. Partridge/*Catch Phrases* suggests that the initial phrase 'neat but not gaudy' was established by c 1800, though in 1631 there had been the similar 'Comely, not gaudy'. Then variations were introduced – as by John Ruskin, writing in the *Architectural Magazine* (November 1838): 'That admiration of the "neat but gaudy" which is commonly reported to have influenced the devil when he painted his tail pea green.' Indeed, Partridge cites: 'Neat, but not gaudy, as the monkey said, when he painted his tail sky blue' and '. . . painted his bottom pink and tied up his tail with pea-green.'

'Never chase girls or buses. There will (always) be another one coming along soon'

Partridge/*Catch Phrases* dates this from the 1920s and derives it from the early US version with 'streetcars' instead of 'buses'. Compare this allusion to the saying by Derick Heathcoat-Amory when Chancellor of the Exchequer (1958–60): 'There are three things not worth running for – a bus, a woman or a new economic panacea; if you wait a bit another one will come along.'

'Night, night, sleep tight, mind that the fleas don't bite'

Or 'Good night...mind the fleas and bugs don't bite.' Nursery traditional.

'It's nourishment I want, not punishment'

Said by a Lancastrian woman in her eighties, when asked why she had never married. Quoted in 1985.

'Oh arr...'

A noncommittal response to something said that is considered unlikely or preposterous or dubious. Compare 'I hear you', a Scots expression meaning that a remark is not worth considering or is untrue or is certainly not going to be responded to.

'It's dark/black over Bill's/Will's mother's way...'

Paul Beale in his revision of Partridge/*Catch Phrases* mentions the expression 'It's a bit black over *Bill's* mother's' (referring to the weather, when rain threatens) and gives an East Midlands source. H S Middleton of Llanyblodwel, Shropshire, formerly of Aylestone Park, Leicester, and whose brother was called Bill, wrote to say how, in the early 1920s, a certain Len Moss had looked through the sitting-room window in the direction of Mr Middleton's home and said, 'It looks black over Bill's mother's.' Was this the origin of the phrase (which sometimes occurs elsewhere as 'over *Will's* mother's way')?

All I was able to tell Mr Middleton was that in 1930, the erudite journal *Notes and Queries* carried a query about this phrase in the form 'It looks pretty black over Will's mother's'. It was described as an 'old Sussex' saying. And there was no response. Barry Day of New York, NY, recalled that 'It's a bit black over Bill's mother's' used to be said a great deal by *his* mother when he was growing up in

Derbyshire. 'It was always said ironically,' he added. 'So I can confirm its Midlands usage.'

I first heard about it on a London radio phone-in (June 1990), in the form, 'It looks like rain . . . over Will's mother's way.' In *Verbatim* (Autumn 1993), Alan Major discussed a number of 'Kentish sayings' and included, 'Out Will's mother's way', meaning 'somewhere else, in the distance, on the horizon'. Major adds: 'Who Will's mother was is unknown, but there are several similar expressions, with word variations, used in other English counties. In Gloucestershire, the expression is "It's dark over our Bill's Mum's mind."'

The Revd P W Gallup of Winchester wrote that he had traced the saying in eleven counties and commented on its age: 'I have friends in their late eighties [in 1994] who as children knew it well from their parents and say that it was then widely known and used. This suggests that the saying has been used at least by several generations.'

'Putting his puddings out for treacle'

In May 1994, Teresa Gorman MP accused Michael Heseltine of disloyalty to Prime Minister John Major by saying that he was 'putting his puddings out for treacle'. Mrs Gorman subsequently explained her expression to Alan Watkins in the *Independent on Sunday* (12 June 1994): ' [It] was used in our neighbourhood about any woman considered to be putting herself forward for attention – or suspected of paying the tradesmen's bills in "kind"!'

'Play with fire, pee in the bed'

A taunt to a child. My wife remembers it from Buckinghamshire in the 1950s and still finds it inexplicable.

'(And) the same to you with (brass) knobs on!'

'With knobs on' simply means 'generous, embellished'. Partridge/*Slang* suggests that this was known by 1910. In 1987, Margaret Walsh of Auckland, New Zealand, told me of this baroque version: 'Same to you with brass fittings and a self-starter.'

'Something old, something new, something borrowed, something blue'

This superstitious phrase listing the traditional components of a bride's wedding apparel does not seem to have been recorded before 1883, though some of the individual

components are certainly older. Blueness expressing trueness is mentioned by Ben Jonson in *Cynthia's Revels* (1601) and by Chaucer (*c* 1390). Walter Redfern, *Clichés and Coinages* (1989) simply calls the expression 'a motto for brides, stand-up comedians, and many writers'.

'Stop picking your nose – you've had your breakfast'

Said by an RAF corporal and quoted by the father of Alice Wood (May 1985).

'They're as much use as a chocolate kettle'

Phil Read of Stoke-on-Trent added to our stock of colourful expressions with this overheard remark at a Port Vale football match. It was after the team had let slip another opportunity to score. Quoted in July 1986.

'A thousand a year'

Said when offering the last portion of food, last sandwich or last cake on a plate. Current in the 1950s, this saying now seems to promise rather slight remuneration for accepting the offer. Iona Opie and Moira Tatem in *A Dictionary of Superstitions* (1992) find various benefits linked to taking the last piece of food on a plate. Their earliest is a 'Lancashire legend' recalled in 1873. From 1923, in Kent: 'The person who, uninvited, takes the last slice of bread and butter from the plate will die unmarried. But the person who takes the last slice upon invitation will have a handsome spouse and an income of thousands amounting to the number of people at the table.'

'Throws his money about like a man with no arms'

The traditional way of describing a mean person.

'The top brick off the chimney'

In 1985, Denis Thatcher, husband of the then prime minister Margaret Thatcher, was quoted as having said: 'I like everything my beloved wife likes. If she wants to buy the top brick of St Paul's, then I would buy it.'

Partridge/*Slang* suggests that the phrase 'to give someone the top brick off the chimney' means 'to be the acme of generosity, with implication that foolish spoiling, or detriment to the donor would result, as in "his parents'd give that boy the..." or "she's that soft-hearted, she'd give you..." 'Partridge's reviser, Paul Beale, who inserted this entry, commented that he had heard the phrase in the early 1980s but that it was probably in use much earlier.

Indeed, when Anthony Trollope was standing for parliament in 1868, he described a seat at Westminster as 'the highest object of ambition to every educated Englishman' and 'the top brick of the chimney'. In *Nanny Says*, Grenfell and Casson's collection of nanny sayings (1972), is included, 'Very particular we are – it's top brick off the chimney or nothing.'

Presumably, Denis Thatcher was reworking this saying for his own ends. Unconsciously, he may also have been conflating it with another kind of reference, such as is found in Charles Dickens, *Martin Chuzzlewit*, Chapter 38 (1844): 'He would as soon have thought of the cross upon the top of St Paul's Cathedral taking note of what he did... as of Nadgett's being engaged in such an occupation.'

"Twas ever thus'

An exclamation meaning almost the same as the modern 'So what's new?' It does not occur in Shakespeare or the Bible. In fact, the only examples I have turned up so far are: as the first line of 'Disaster' by C S Calverley (*d* 1884): ''Twas ever thus from childhood's hour!' (this is a parody of lines from Thomas Moore's 'The Fire Worshippers' in *Lalla Rookh* (1817): 'Oh! ever thus from childhood's hour!'); and as the title, ''Twas Ever Thus', given to the parody of the same poem by Henry S Leigh (1837–83). His version begins, 'I never rear'd a young gazelle.'

'Two six, to do a'

Mr E Pettinger of Elsrickle, Lanarkshire, inquired about a saying 'which was common among RAF ground staff when I was serving between 1945 and 1948. It was said when help was required in opening or closing the big hangar doors – "Two Six on the hangar doors!" I can still visualise the response following the shout. One had to stop what one was doing and help to push the enormous sliding doors. Partridge/*Slang* dates it from 1930 and gives the definition 'to do something very speedily and promptly'.

Compare 'one-two, one-two', which a military person might bark with the same intention. Possibly from gun-drill – the number of a command in an instruction booklet?

'Up the wooden hill/stairs to Bedfordshire'

Originally a nursery euphemism, I think this has become part of grown-up 'golf-club slang', as someone once termed it – ie a conversational cliché. Sir Hugh Casson and Joyce Grenfell included it in their *Nanny Says* (1972), together with 'Come on, up wooden hill, down sheet lane.' 'Up the Wooden Hill to Bedfordshire' was the title of the very first song recorded by Vera Lynn, in 1936. The 'bed – fordshire' joke occurs in a synopsis of *Ali Baba and the Forty Thieves; or, Harlequin and the Magic Donkey* staged at the Alexandra Theatre, Liverpool, in 1868. Indeed, as so often, Jonathan Swift found it even earlier. In *Polite Conversation* (1738), the Colonel says, 'I'm going to the Land of Nod.' Neverout replies: 'Faith, I'm for *Bedfordshire*.' But then again, the poet Charles Cotton had used it in 1665 and Apperson finds 'Bedfordshire' = 'bed' in a play by Middleton in 1608.

Jim Sweeney, the comedy performer, recalled that not only would his mother say the above, his father would set off early to bed with the words: 'I will arise and go now, and go to Innisfree' (courtesy of W B Yeats).

'What a name to go to bed with'

Partridge/*Slang* has 'a nice name to go to bed with' – meaning 'an ugly name' – dating from 1887 and compares the French expression, '*Un nom à coucher dehors*'.

Mrs D M Heigham of Aldershot, Hampshire, wrote: 'It was New Year's Eve 1943. I was a Cypher Officer WRNS on watch at midnight. I was introduced to a man called Worthington Edridge. "Oh," I said, "what a name to go to bed with" (current remark at the time). He said, "Nobody asked you." I don't think you can beat that for a put-down.'

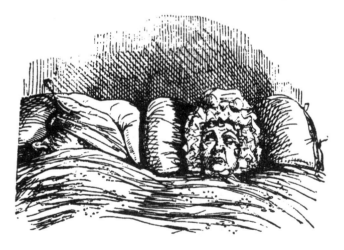

'Wet and warm'

On being offered a drink, one might say, 'I don't mind what it is, so long as it's wet and warm.' Almost a conversational cliché. H L Mencken in his *Dictionary of Quotations* (1942) cites a 'Dutch proverb': 'Coffee has two virtues: it is wet and warm.' Pat Tomalin of Gussage All Saints wrote in May 1992 to describe how in Kenya c 1950, 'We used to say, "Wet and warm, like a honeymoon in Aden".'

'What's that got to do with the Prince of Wales?'

Meaning, 'What you've just said is irrelevant'. Told to me on an LBC radio phone-in, London, in June 1990, but otherwise untraced and unconfirmed. And which Prince of Wales is being talked about? Compare, however, 'What has that to do with Bacchus?' which *Brewer's Dictionary of Phrase and Fable* finds in classical literature. Partridge/*Catch Phrases* has 'What's that got to do with the price of eggs?' as being of American origin. Sir John Bjelke-Peterson, once Premier of Queensland, was reported in *The Australian* (1 May 1985) as saying of something he thought was irrelevant, 'That's got nothing to do with the price of butter.'

'When it's brown it's done, when it's black it's buggered'

On cooking. Peter Cotterill of Doncaster wrote to the *Guardian* (28 March 1987) and quoted his Lancashire mum to this effect.

DVWPXYZ

My maternal grandfather, Arthur Gleave of Liverpool, is fondly remembered for his many little sayings, many of the trick or riddle type. When driving past a cemetery, he would say, 'That's where they bury the deaf and dumb, you know.' After a pause, one was supposed to ask, 'How do you know they do that?' And he would ritually reply, 'We're all deaf and dumb when we're dead.' Driving along a wiggly road in the country would always bring forth the comment, 'I think they must have made this bit after they'd had a good lunch.'

And so on and so on. He – or perhaps it was his wife – also used to end written or spoken communications with some such message as 'I'll see you Thursday. D V W P X Y Z' You were supposed to be baffled. 'D V', naturally, was 'Deo volente [God willing]'; 'W P' was 'Weather Permitting'; – and 'X Y Z'? Just for good measure.

As a token acknowledgement of the number of domestic catchphrases that are of a riddle-like nature – particularly the meaningless ones – here is a brief selection:

'How many beans make five?'

A joke riddle, but also uttered as an answer to an impossible question (along the lines of 'How long is a piece of string?' etc). Miss Alice Lloyd was singing a music-hall song in November 1898 which contained these lines:

> You say you've never heard
> How many beans make five?

It's time you knew a thing or two –
You don't know you're alive!

Miss M L King of London SW3 told me that the correct
answer is: 'Two in each hand and one in the mouth.'

'Where was Moses when the light went out?'

This 'almost proverbial' riddle (as the Opies call it in *The
Lore and Language of Schoolchildren*, 1959) may have a
precise answer:

Q Where was Moses when the light went out?
A In the dark.

The Opies found that in *The Riddler's Oracle*, *c* 1821. Miss
M L King (as above) said the answer 'according to my
brother in the twenties was: "Running round the table with
his shirt hanging out".'
    The 1968 film *Where Were You When the Lights Went
Out?* was inspired by the great New York blackout of 1965
when the electricity supply failed and, it was popularly
believed, the birthrate shot up nine months later. The phrase
echoes our riddle, possibly an old music-hall song, and
perhaps also a nonsense rhyme (of American origin, I think)
– 'Where was Moses when the light went out?/Down in the
cellar eating sauerkraut.'

'Why is a mouse when it spins?'

I mentioned a nonsensical riddle on Channel 4's
Countdown programme in 1987 and was amazed at the
response I had from viewers. The riddle went:

Q Why is a mouse when it spins?

and the suggested answer was:

A The higher, the fewer.

Most people remembered it being told to them by teasing parents in the 1920s and 30s. John Mack of Surbiton suggested that it originated in repartee between Jasper Maskelyne and Oswald Williams in magic shows at the St George's Hall in Langham Place, London, in about 1930. If not originated, he says, it was certainly much used by them.

Mrs Jean E French of Finchampstead suggested that it might not be nonsensical if you substituted the word 'when' for 'why' in posing the riddle. From this I wondered whether it had anything to with 'Hickory, dickory, dock, the mouse ran up the clock, the clock struck one, the mouse fell down . . . '

A variation of the riddle (which doesn't help either) is:

Q Why is a mouse when it's spinning its web?
A Because the more the fewer the quicker.

Other viewers raked up these equally nonsensical riddles:

Q How is a man when he's out?
A The sooner he does, the much.

Q What is the difference between a duck?
A One of its legs is both the same.

Q Which would you rather, or go fishing? [*or* swimming/hunting?]
A One rode a horse and the other rhododendron.

This last may not be a riddle at all and the answer may belong elsewhere. Partridge/*Slang* gives 'What shall we do, or go fishing' as a 'trick elaboration' of the straightforward 'What shall we do now?' (It is quoted in Dorothy L Sayers, *The Nine Tailors*, 1934.) Compare: 'Which would you rather be – or a wasp?'

'Why is a raven like a writing desk?'

In *Alice's Adventures in Wonderland* (1865) by Lewis Carroll, the Hatter poses this riddle at the Mad Hatter's Tea-Party, but Carroll stated positively that there was no answer. Nevertheless, various people have tried to supply one:

'a quill' – what a raven and a writing desk would have had in common in the last century (Christopher Brown of Portswood, Southampton).

'they both begin with the letter R' (Leo Harris).

'because it can produce a few notes, tho they are very flat; and it is never put with the wrong end in front' – these were Lewis Carroll's own possible solutions (1896 edition).

'because the notes for which they are noted are not noted for being musical notes' (Sam Loyd) .

'Edgar Allan Poe' – he wrote on both a raven and a writing desk (Sam Loyd).

'because bills and tales (tails) are among their characteristics; because they both stand on their legs; conceal their steels (steals); and ought to be made to shut up' (Sam Loyd).

'because it slopes with a flap' (A Cyril Pearson).

'because there is a "B" in "both"' (Dr E V Rieu).

(Some of these solutions are included in *The Annotated Alice*, ed Martin Gardner, 1960.)

In *The Yeoman of the Guard* (1888), W S Gilbert also poses a riddle without an answer. Jack Point, the Strolling Jester, asks: 'Why [is] a cook's brain-pan...like an overwound clock?' but he is interrupted before the solution can be given. 'Just my luck,' he exclaims, 'my best conundrum wasted!'

Ian Bradley in his *Annotated Gilbert and Sullivan* (Vol 2, 1984) notes that Sir Henry Lytton once asked Gilbert what the answer to his conundrum was and was told by the librettist that he would leave it in his will. Needless to say, when he died, it wasn't there. The truth is that Gilbert had never bothered about answering his own riddle.'

'Why is a sheet of foolscap like a lazy dog?'

To restore sanity, here is an old riddle which does have an answer. The answer is:

A A sheet of foolscap is an ink lined plain. An inclined plain is a slope up. A slow pup is a lazy dog.

'Willie, Willie, Harry, Stee...'

Not a riddle but a mnemonic. A mention on *Quote...Unquote* of the rhyme for remembering the order of the reigns of the kings and queens of England resulted in many requests for copies. So here is the anonymous composition which was probably in existence by 1900.

Willie, Willie, Harry, Stee,
Harry, Dick, John, Harry Three.

One, Two, Three Neds, Richard Two.
Henries Four, Five, Six...then who?

Edward Four, Five, Dick the Bad.
Harries twain and Ned the Lad.

Mary, Bessie, James the Vain.
Charlie, Charlie, James Again.

William and Mary, Anna Gloria,
Four Georges, William and Victoria.

Len Robinson of Benfleet, Essex, said that at Brigg Grammar School in 1933, he learned the jingle thus far, with the additional couplet:

Edward Seventh next, and then
George the Fifth in 1910.

'In 1936,' he said, 'we made two successive amendments.' Since then, for the benefit of his children (and grandchildren) he had brought the lines up to date:

In '36 came Edward Eight
Who, in that year, did abdicate.

George Six followed. At his death
In '52, Elizabeth.

Another version of the post-Victoria reigns is:

Edward Seven, George again
Edward Eight gave up his reign.

George Six, he of gentle mien
Elizabeth Two, God Save the Queen.

A 'strongly Anglophile' American also rhymed Edward VIII/George VI thus:

Eddie Eight went helter-skelter,
Georgie reigned from a bomb-proof shelter.

A Bird in the Hand Spoils the Broth

As must have become apparent by now, a proverbial strain is markedly apparent in a majority of domestic catch-phrases. Many family sayings are simply proverbs of one sort or another. But what sort? So many proverbs are downright peculiar and/or unhelpful. Far from expressing a universal truth they offer observations that are obscure, incomprehensible or just plain odd. And then there are the madeup ones, which are much more jolly. A brief selection.

'No one ever died of a bad smell'

Told to me by Katharine Whitehorn but not broadcast, for some reason.

'A brownish bird in a tallish tree/Means sorrow – or joy – for somebody'

Katharine's husband, Gavin Lyall, the novelist, got so fed up with country proverbs that he invented this all-purpose one.

'Rain in June keeps all in tune'

In *Love from Nancy: The Letters of Nancy Mitford* (1993), reference is made to a letter to Nancy from Diana Mosley (dated 10 June 1946): 'About the time of the [V Day] procession I saw Baker [the gamekeeper at Crowood] & said terribly wet. Yes he replied, his mind on farming, but they do say Rain in June keeps all in tune.'

They do, indeed. An earlier form of the proverb (recorded in 1846) is: 'A good leak in June/Sets all in tune.

'A mackerel sky is very wet – or very dry'

Sian Phillips chose this to illustrate the unhelpfulness of weather proverbs. Mrs Barbara Williams of Plymouth said that the version she grew up with was, ' Mackerel sky, mackerel sky/Neither wet, neither dry.' Apperson finds any number of explanations as to what a mackerel sky foretells and none of them is very helpful. For example from West Somerset (1886): 'Mackerel-sky! not much wet, not much dry.'

'Empty vessels carry no cargo'

Believed to have been manufactured for a *New Statesman* competition.

'The only difference between men and boys is the price of their toys'

This modern proverbial expression has been credited both to Liberace and to Joyce Brothers in the US. In the UK, there is a difference: writer Derek Robinson talking in 1990 about the making of a TV version of his novel *Piece of Cake* said he noticed that everyone was fascinated by the Spitfire aircraft. All work would come to a stop whenever they were being used. A technician standing by remarked, 'You can tell the men from the boys by the size of their toys.'

'I'm not as Irish as I'm cabbage looking'

Gemma O'Connor selected this Irish proverb. Also 'I don't boil my cabbage twice' and 'One black-backed beetle recognizes another black-backed beetle' (ie 'It takes one to know one.')

'You never know the minute'

According to Ken Bruce, the disc-jockey, this lugubrious sentiment is the sort you intone at a Scottish funeral.

'Don't sit there like Lord Kehoy'

Ken Bruce's mother used to say it to him, and he still doesn't know what she meant.

'You winter them, you summer them, you winter them again, and then you say hello'

Hunter Davies recalled this Lake District saying which expresses the attitude of Cumbrian folk to newcomers.

'Today the party has come to our street'

Bernard Bresslaw claimed this to be a Russian proverb, but offered no explanation. He also said his mother-in-law had a saying, 'Yes, live horse and you'll get grass' – in response to people saying if you do such and such, everything will come all right. Partridge/*Slang* has, rather, 'Live horse! And thou shalt have grass' and glosses it as, 'Well, let's wait and see! Later on, we'll see!' Swift had it in *Polite Conversation* (1738).

'The road to the chapel is icy, so is the road to the tavern, but I will walk carefully'

Sir Peter Ustinov proffered this Russian proverb, together with the more penetrable 'Love thy neighbour but build a fence' and 'Love God but don't neglect the Devil.'

'It is in vain to look for yesterday's fish in the house of the otter'

A helpful Hindu proverb quoted by Simon Brett, who also relished the fine German, 'A fart has no nose.'

'Trust in the Lord...and tie up your camel'

My wife told me this one, having heard it in a business context. No other source, I am afraid.

'Do not tie your shoes in a melon field or adjust your hat under a plum tree if you wish to avoid suspicion'

A proverb recorded by Claud Cockburn in *I Claud* (1967). He claimed it was Chinese.

'Seeing is believing – but feeling's better proof!'

An anonymous correspondent in Hampshire wrote to say that this was 'my Irish grandmother's version' of the more familiar 'Seeing is believing.' Apperson finds the well known first half expressed in Plautus. It was known in English by 1639 and is also reflected in John 20:29.

The longer version is sometimes known in America as 'Seeing is believing but feeling is the truth'.

'There were more holes in his pocket than the one where he put his own hand'

Quoted by George Eliot in *Silas Marner* (1861).

'The dogs bark but the caravan passes by'

Meaning, 'Critics make a noise but, never mind, it does not last.' Sir Peter Hall, the theatre director, was given to quoting this 'Turkish proverb' when attacks were made on him in the mid-1970s. In *Within a Budding Grove* – the 1924 translation of Marcel Proust's *A l'Ombre des Jeunes Filles en Fleurs* (1918) – C K Scott Moncrieff has: 'the fine Arab proverb, "The dogs may bark; the caravan goes on!"' Truman Capote entitled a book *The Dogs Bark: Public People and Private Places* (1974).

'It's no use going to bed early to save candles, if the result be twins'

A Chinese proverb quoted by John Julius Norwich.

'You cannot prevent the birds of sadness from flying over your head, but you can prevent them from nesting in your hair'

Yet another Chinese proverb, quoted by Dillie Keane.

'He who drowneth his brother cannot blame the tiger'

John Peel, the disc-jockey, admitted to having invented this very useful all-purpose 'Persian proverb'.

'He digs deepest who deepest digs'

Roger Woddis won a *New Statesman* competition with this one in 1969.

'It's a flat fish that seeks shallow water'

Max Stafford-Clark chose this proverb and described it as an excellent conversation stopper.

'Just because there's snow on the roof, it doesn't mean the fire's out inside'

Peter Jones recalled what men say when their hair goes

prematurely white. A relatively modern coinage, I think, and probably American.

'No good deed goes unpunished'

This is a consciously ironic rewriting of the older expression 'No *bad* deed goes unpunished' and has been attributed to Oscar Wilde, but remains unverified. Joe Orton recorded it in his diary for 13 June 1967: 'Very good line George [Greeves] came out with at dinner: "No good deed ever goes unpunished."' James Agate in *Ego 3* (for 25 January 1938) stated: '[Isidore Leo] Pavia was in great form today: "Every good deed brings its own punishment."'

'Even a short leg reaches the ground'

I was once assured that this had won a *New Statesman* competition for Dr J Walter Heydecker, but Lyndon Irving is also credited with 'No leg's too short to reach the ground' in the *Statesman's* 'Meaningless Proverb' quest of 1967. I have no opinion on the matter.

'Every time a sheep bleats it loses a nibble'

H L Mencken's *Dictionary of Quotations* (1947) has this as an English proverb in the form, 'Every time the sheep bleats it loses a mouthful' and 'apparently borrowed from the Italian and familiar since the seventeenth century'. *CODP* finds a version in 1599 and seems to prefer the form 'A bleating sheep loses a bite', explaining it as, 'Opportunities are missed through too much chatter.'

'You can lead a horse to the water, but you can't force rhubarb'

An example of what happens when you rub two well-known proverbs together. As also: 'Too many cooks make a white', 'Two blacks don't make a wrong', 'Marry in haste; try, try again', 'A bird in the hand spoils the broth.'

'When one door closes, another door closes'

A cynical modern variant of the older 'When one door closes, another door opens' (which *CODP* has by 1586). I recall being told the modern one (perhaps from America) in about 1969.

'It takes seventy-two muscles to frown, but only thirteen to smile'

Heaven knows where this originated. It is quoted by Celia Haddon in *The Yearbook of Comfort and Joy* (1991). As for 'When the rain rains and the goose winketh, little wots the gosling what the goose thinketh' – Celia claimed this was a local proverb from Ilminster in Somerset, but did not find a place for it in any of her Yearbooks. Nor, oddly, the advice to young women: 'He that's cooled with an apple and heated with an egg over me shall never spread his leg.'

'Mad men and lame men copulate best'

A truly peculiar proverb quoted in Walter Redfern, *Clichés and Coinages* (1989).

'Trees are tall but they do not reach to the sky'

Is this one of those actual Russian folk proverbs, or a made-up one? And what does it mean? John Colville quoted Winston Churchill as saying 'The trees do not grow up to the sky' on 6 January 1953 in a situation where he seemed to be recommending a 'wait and see' policy. In other words, 'Trees may be tall, but they're not that tall.' Later in the same year, on 9 November, in his speech to the Lord Mayor's Banquet, Churchill said: 'Another old saying comes back to my mind which I have often found helpful or at least comforting. I think it was Goethe who said, "The trees do not grow up to the sky." I do not know whether he would have said that if he had lived through this frightful twentieth century where so much we feared was going to happen did actually happen. All the same it is a thought which should find its place in young as well as old brains.'

Goethe? So perhaps it isn't Russian after all.

'Pissing in his shoe makes no man warm for long'

Included by W H Auden and Christopher Isherwood in *Letters from Iceland* (1937). I wonder whether they didn't make it up? After all, in *The Faber Book of Aphorisms* (1964) (which Auden edited with Kronenburger), 'Every man likes the smell of his own farts' is described as of Icelandic origin. But later, when Auden wrote in *The Dyer's Hand* (1962): 'Most people enjoy the sight of their own handwriting as they enjoy the smell of their own farts', he passed it off as his own.

'Rice cakes are best made by the rice-cake maker'

Anthony Thwaite quoted this Japanese proverb, which is sensible enough. Also two Arab proverbs: 'He who sits on a cactus may seek for a cushion' and 'We traded in shrouds; people stopped dying' – the ultimate in hard luck stories. Compare this last with the rhyme:

> If I sold shrouds
>   No one would die;
> If I sold lamps then in the sky
>   The sun, in my despite,
>   Would shine all night.

which is quoted by James Agate in *Ego 5* (1942) (entry for 4 November 1941), in relation to the question of luck in his journalistic struggles. He does not say where it came from.

'Somebody has to bury the undertaker'

Winston Fletcher, the advertising guru, dealt with the passing off of impressive-sounding proverbs in his seminal work *Meetings, Meetings* (1983). He quoted a past master of the genre, Jeremy Bullmore, one-time chairman of J Walter Thompson, as saying the above – and also: 'It may not be the man who saws the logs who needs the fire.'

He quoted Freddie Tarrant, a head-hunter, as saying: 'After all, a door has to be closed before it can be opened.' And Joseph Berkman, restaurant owner, produced the superb: 'As we always say in Austria, those who have butter on their heads don't walk in the sun.'

I'm Mrs de Winter Now!

Closing your eyes and tapping your heels together three times (like Dorothy in *The Wizard of Oz*) may be one way of keeping your spirits up, but how do other people manage? What quotable personal mottoes, meaningful proverbs and verbal talispersons do people carry about with them, and say to themselves, when the going gets tough? My choice, already quoted, would be Dr Johnson's advice on dealing with distress ('Consider, Sir, how insignificant this will appear a twelvemonth hence'). Or, André Maurois's observation on Balzac: 'In defeat he thought only of future victories.'

Charles Osborne related what the poet Philip Larkin had told him. When people were ganging up on him, Larkin would draw himself up to his full height and say to himself the line from Daphne du Maurier's *Rebecca*: '*I'm* Mrs de Winter now!'

'Frenchmen, one more effort if we are to become Republicans!'

The jazz singer George Melly admitted to quoting this line from the Marquis de Sade. It was the heading of a pamphlet he wrote when he thought the French Revolution was going the wrong way. 'Now this has such a lovely, meaningless ring to it, that I find for instance that whenever I should do out a drawer or sit down and write an article, I say this.'

'Alone I did it'

Robert Stephens, the actor, said he quoted a line he had once delivered in the title role of Shakespeare's *Coriolanus*. In other words, he did it *his* way.

'En avant!'

Maria St Just was an actress friend of the playwright Tennessee Williams. Her book of letters from Williams – *Five O'Clock Angel* – was published by André Deutsch in 1991: 'When I first met Tennessee, he was an extremely shy, very vulnerable and enchanting creature, and remained so to the end of his life. He never lost his shyness, his enthusiasm, nor his courage and strength, although he went through the most incredible hoops of agony, disappointment and frustration, and a terrible feeling of failure. His great cry was always "En avant!" When my daughter was born and we asked him to be the godfather, he wrote, "Buy her a silver christening cup and please engrave it with my motto, 'En Avant'. I put it after every entry in my journal, no matter how things have stopped: the courage to go on is a lot in life."'

'Dread one day at a time'

Celia Haddon said she liked adapting high-minded mottoes to something more practical. Alcoholics Anonymous said 'Just live one day at a time', but she preferred what she once saw in the Peanuts cartoon strip: 'I've got a new philosophy. I'm just going to dread one day at a time.'

'It is better to light a candle than to grumble about the dark'

When Bryan Magee has to bestir himself, he said, 'I give myself little talkings to' – and quoted this Jewish proverb.

'Too much is not enough'

Nina Myskow, the journalist, said her motto was 'Shop till you drop', but she also treasured something given to her by her friend Renate, the one-time wife of Elton John. Once, Renate bought twelve identical pairs of shoes from Beverley Feldman of Hollywood and insisted that Nina should share in this extravagance. Hand-tooled in the leather of the sole of one pair was, appropriately, 'Too much is not enough.'

'Dignity... always dignity'

When the disc-jockey Ken Bruce's record-playing equipment starts to go wrong and chaos invades his studio, he said he likes to quote a line from the film *Singin' in the Rain*. Gene Kelly recalls earlier, terrible times playing in cheap dives and proffers this motto.

'There is no more pleasant sight than to see a good friend fall from a rooftop'

Max Stafford-Clark admitted to enjoying the bad critical notices of friends of his who are also stage directors. It made him think of the comment usually attributed to Confucius.

'Keep breathing'

Sian Phillips said that, when under stress, she quotes the words of Sophie Tucker.

'Courage!'

Peter Jones is very nervous on first nights so he says this in French – 'because it sounds better in that language'. Also: 'They must go forward who have no retreat!'

'Cheer up, old heart, you've known worse things than this'

Katharine Whitehorn's father would address her in Greek, of which this is a translation. But she is also encouraged by journalistic mottoes of the type spoken by editors: 'Don't get it right, get it written' and 'Don't want it good, want it Tuesday.' (The last of these also appears in showbiz contexts.

Denis Norden was quoted in the *Mail on Sunday*, 16 January 1994, as noting, 'There's an old showbiz line about the producer saying, "I don't want it good, I want it Monday".')

'A l'oeuvre, mon bon! [To work, my good fellow]'

Frederic Raphael said he quoted what Henry James used to write in his notebook when he felt lazy.

'Do the next thing'

Stage director Peter Wood said that he was encouraged by the motto that is written up in Audley End house. The Beatles, when they were together, used to have a similar preoccupation with what they termed 'The Next Big Thing' – the next project or all-consuming interest.

'Where McGregor sits *is* the head o' the table'

Broadcaster Sue McGregor could take heart from this motto, if she needed it. The fable has it that McGregor, who was head of the Scottish clan, was invited to an important function. At dinner, his host apologized for not placing him at the head of the table. To which McGregor responded, 'Where McGregor sits *is* the head o' the table.' There are various versions of this. In a letter from Lord Chesterfield to Lord Huntingdon (19 May 1756), Chesterfield quoted 'what the late Duke of Somerset [said] absurdly, when accidentally placed below himself one day at table, *the best place is wherever I sit*.' A footnote to the 1923 publication of this letter states: 'The Highland Chief, The McNab, also said: "Where the McNab sits, there is the Head of the Table."'

'Well, we's all live till we dee, unless dogs worries us'

Kit Blease of Wallasey wrote: 'This was used by my mother – a Yorkshire West Riding lady – usually after some minor disaster in the home.' Anne Gledhill of Mirfield, West Yorkshire, added: 'It was part of my background, too (born and brought up in Dewsbury in the West Riding).' Her version: 'We shall live till we dee – if t'dogs doesn't worry us' (the second part given an ironic twist). Other remarks expressing a philosophical endurance: 'It won't always be dark at six', 'The harder it rains, the sooner the shower's over' and 'There's many a worse job at sea.'

'Us never deed a winter yet, Us allus sprutted up in Spring [We never died a winter yet, we always sprouted up in Spring]'

Phyllis Jessop of Kingsclere, Berkshire, wrote: 'My Yorkshire mother-in-law used to quote her neighbour as saying this.

(Also she would say if an article of clothing was badly made: "It fits like a stocking on a chicken's lip.")'

'When she hands you a dishcloth, blow your nose on it and hand it back'

Advice given by a friend to David Cookson of Witternsen, North Humberside, when he was about to get married.

'Is it kind? Is it true? Is it necessary?'

The widow of Edward Wilson, the Antarctic explorer, had these words printed over her mantelshelf to remind herself to curb a sharp tongue. Mrs D M Thomas of Hinckley, Leicestershire, said she found this information in George Seaver's book *Edward Wilson of the Antarctic* (1933/63) and then in *Gaudy Night* by Dorothy L Sayers, where it is spoken (with the first two questions reversed) by that arch-quoter, Lord Peter Wimsey. But where did the saying come from originally?

It bears a certain resemblance to part of 'The Four Way Test of the things we think, say or do' that American Rotarians devised in 1931: 'Is it the truth? Is it *fair*? Will it be beneficial to all concerned?' But I think a more likely origin lies in a poem called 'The Three Gates' and said to have been written by Beth Day in 1855 'after the Arabian':

> If you are tempted to reveal
> A tale to you someone has told
> About another, make it pass,
> Before you speak, three gates of gold.
> These narrow gates: First, 'Is it true?'
> Then, 'Is it needful?' In your mind
> Give truthful answer. And the next
> Is last and narrowest, 'Is it kind?'
> And if to reach your lips at last
> It passes through these gateways three,
> Then you may tell the tale, nor fear
> What the result of speech may be.

'Oh, well, what's life to a man whose wife's a widow!'

Avril Fox of Market Weston, Suffolk, recalled a favourite motto uttered when the going was bad by 'a very Welsh transport manager in a Cotswold milk-processing depot in which I worked as a girl.'